ANCIENT EGYPTIAN CELESTIAL HEALING

THE SOURCE CODES FOR HIGH FREQUENCY

ANCIENT EGYPTIAN CELESTIAL HEALING

THE SOURCE CODES FOR HIGH FREQUENCY

TRACEY ASH

FINDHORN PRESS

Published in 2015 by Findhorn Press, Scotland

ISBN 978-1-84409-663-3

Edited by Michael Hawkins
Photos by Tracey Ash Film and Photo Archives,
except for: *p. 30 Peter Hermes Furian / Wikipedia; p. 116 Shooarts;
p. 117 Maximus 256; p. 118 Subbotina / Lightwave; p. 141 Alphaspirit.*
Cover design by Maria Eisl, *www.studioeisl.com*
Interior design by Damian Keenan
Printed & bound in the EU

Published by

Findhorn Press

117-121 High Street,

Forres IV36 1AB,

Scotland, UK

t +44 (0)1309 690582

f +44 (0)131 777 2711

e info@findhornpress.com

www.findhornpress.com

Contents

BOOK **TWO**

Disclaimer

The information in this book is given in good faith and is neither intended to diagnose any physical or mental condition nor to serve as a substitute for informed medical advice or care.
Please contact your health professional for medical advice and treatment. Neither author nor publisher can be held liable by any person for any loss or damage whatsoever which may arise from the use of this book or any of the information therein.

'For every love story

that makes you

and the world

more magnificent

every day.'

Foreword

*A*ncient Egyptian Celestial Healing is a simple, transformation and aware-ness super-technology for the twenty-first century. This book is for indi-viduals passionate about the essential, 'how to', on new transformation and hu-manity frontiers for magnificent self and world change contribution.

This book travels with you to enter The Source Codes – a high-frequency miracle-resource for powering intelligence and excellence. *Celestial Healing* exposes scientific and historical evidence on ancient knowledge technologies that accelerate miracles in your life and world, where it matters most.

The first secret is practical and simple, the 'how to' on transformation and peace; this is the purpose of every self-help book on this planet! The second se-cret, the bigger secret is 'how to' switch on a high frequency for solid foundations of outstanding potential.

- *THE SOURCE CODES IS THE BIGGEST AND MOST IMPORTANT SECRET RESOURCE TO UNLOCK IN LIFE.*
- *IGNITE NEW HIGH-FREQUENCY TRANSFORMATION AND MANIFESTATION FRONTIERS FOR THE GREATEST STORIES OF MAGNIFICENCE.*
- *THIS IS THE NEXT TEMPLATE OF EVOLUTION INTO A NEW WORLD.*

So many people are asking how to consciously and responsibly switch on high frequency. This is the book to read to overwrite and delete elite power structures, limited thinking and conspiracy theories. It takes you into a new frontier of out-standing human potential, changing your stories to change your world.

You move into authentic transformation and consciousness change, beyond pain cycles that create truly effective positive self and world change. This key is you.

This book documents my stories of discovering The Source Codes during my journeys in Ancient Egypt, to sharing the love and compassion of a new frontier of purpose and generosity at this critical time of urgent world change.

I love my work and the spirit of change that is freedom. I share everything in this book I have learned so far. The more I share the more I learn. The more you share every day the more you learn every day and give beautifully, purposefully and generously in the world you exist in. This is the truest and most impeccable path of healing and spirituality.

Our world urgently needs enduring kindness, truths, integrity, awareness and love that heals and intelligently contributes. These are of course, intellectual concepts but only solid awareness and highest frequency creates this. The new frontiers and possibilities for a better world are based not only in knowledge but the profound wisdom and truth of frequencies shaping the world we exist in.

Here you can truly change your stories and truly transform your world – awakening a new paradigm of time, potential and change at every level of life. I live for and love this work, to hand over the hope of a better world for our future generations and future earth. For those who truly love and care, this journey is the path of the true and selfless hero who shines as awake, positive and loving.

This book reveals essential 'how to' on freeing self from low-frequency toxic stories and slow repeat-toxic cycles so you can build and build positive change into your life. All stories exist, this is real, the secret is to 'know how' to opt out of toxic and often destructive stories that limit you, impact our future, world and humanity.

Elite power structures manufacture crisis after crisis on the largest scale yet; striking inner balance, individual freedom and effective change can be difficult. The key is high frequency. But how if energy levels are low and life is increasingly challenging? What if you could super-empower? What if you could break slow moving, toxic cycles? What if you could super-charge?

It is here you enter incredible journeys of humanity, awareness and action to engage with the stories in life that really matter. This is the path of positive and good, taking awareness and action to the next level. Only then, do you hold the power of positive change to upscale human capacity to love self and world deeply and consciously.

Celestial Healing can help you increase the magnificence and speed of your transformation, to magnify and upscale purpose and action. What could you manifest if you could transform and navigate beyond toxic cycles, crisis mop-up operations and coping strategies that impact quality of life? How would you spend more of your precious time and life force?

Celestial Healing reveals why high frequency should not solely be found in rare moments or meditation bliss, but in life where magnificence really matters. It is time to allow and create more. This is truly outstanding change. This is The

Source Codes truth. *Celestial Healing* reveals how to power up in high frequency and remain powered, to exist purposefully and consciously in all stories.

Since The Arab Spring events of 2011, The Source Codes were revealed during my journeys in Egypt, at major monuments and power sites all around the world. My narratives with encrypted ancient knowledge unlocked simple, high-frequency super-technologies essential for now.

~

This is the insider's knowledge we all need to know for closing down and walking away from cycles of low-frequency toxic stories whoever we are, whatever we do, so we can live as our best self. *Without high-frequency magnificence, we cannot be the change we dream of.*

Without high-frequency magnificence, we do not create the lasting freedom and evolution that is the purpose of the next world phase.

Celestial Healing reveals some of the most essential new 'how to' on super-transformation, super-awareness and super-manifestation. The question from every individual I work with, is always how? This book takes you on journeys to know and enter The Source Codes, to up-scale purpose and potential, to manifest outstanding change in your life and world. The Source Codes expose our ancient cosmic origins and bond.

These super-technologies powerfully reframe your stories of transformation, awareness and magnificence in everyday life to create a better world. Are you driven to discover how to live your life and world beyond the toxic stories that limits every human being on this planet? Are you passionate about positive change and critical contribution? Do you dream of creating magnificent stories for self and especially others? Do you want to know 'how to' live in more magnificent stories?

This book contains many secrets for living a magnificent story so that you can now decide. Your magnificent story is the seed of a new world. This can truly change our world.

~

Since 1999, I have worked with individuals who seek lasting powerful self and world change: often seeking the 'how to', to unlock and maintain magnificent purpose and change again and again. I am always working with intelligent individuals who care deeply about a positive world.

My journey super-accelerated in The Arab Spring events of 2011, during my Return to Light Tours in the ancient monuments of Egypt. Here, The Source Codes were revealed in narratives and these narratives were filmed live, powerfully potent, visible and tangible. These experiences unlocked ancient knowledge on highest frequencies that brings choice and positive change despite, as I have written above, challenging toxic stories and life events.

This led to successful journeys of working with many more individuals in a common bond and vision despite intense, chaotic world events. The seed of Celestial Healing was born. This has led me to work at monumental power sites all around the world and, crucially, has also led me to understand how frequency is essential in monumental transformation and awakening. I have learned to utilize the high-frequency switch for monumental individual and planetary healing despite intense individual and world events.

The Source Codes unlocks and opens a new frontier of super-consciousness and planetary peace of *beyond-wildest-dreams transformation. Celestial Healing* is for individuals who think differently, believe differently, dream differently, who believe positive and good change can be created now. This not only takes vision and courage but highest frequency for action and contribution as warriors and ambassadors of new and positive change.

Even this book's promotional film, recorded in the King's Chamber in November 2014, depicts The Source Codes dancing, in my narrative on why individual and world change is so urgent now. This YouTube film opens the door to witnessing and experiencing first hand, the incredible frequencies that we can now tap into for magnificent and monumental peace and evolution. Every film in my archived collection tells this story.

This story rewrites us beyond duality and pain into the next evolutionary phase.

Ancient Egyptian Celestial Healing explores our cosmic origins and the conspiracy to conceal The Source Codes truths, the archaic super-power of Ancient Egyptian technologies and what the Ancients knew that we no longer have access to. How stories and frequency frame your level of choice and freedom. How to enter The Source Codes to navigate through a minefield of stories, into the magnificence and truths your sovereignty deserves. How you can use The Source Codes to live in increasing high-frequency purpose, awareness and transformation every day. What changes when you enter The Source Codes? What can you expect? Just what can you manifest? Here are three main secrets you will find:

Visions of Super-Change during my travels to earth power sites awakened incredible super-energy technologies that can be understood through cutting-edge science, history and new spirituality in Part One of this book. Simple meditation frameworks and high-frequency practices can be explored in Part Two. Here you learn how to apply Source Codes technologies simply to transform and awaken the best of you in meditation, and living life every moment of every day.

Why The Source Codes are so super-critical in helping you navigate the turbulent earth and humanity changes of these times. Why and how you can manifest incredible transformation and progress for self and world. How super-consciousness can now be unlocked to create incredible new change possibilities. World-class film and photograph archives capture the magic of a new frontier of super-energy to the gateway of new dreams for humanity and earth. See *www. traceyash.com* for blog and YouTube archives.

Celestial Healing transforms and unlocks your magic again and again. No more meditation experiences or transformation breakthroughs that are logged in miniscule episodes or lacklustre silence. Celestial Healing delivers everyday, where it matters, in living and maintaining your magnificence. Celestial Healing ignites awareness, *'know how'* and powerful solutions in your life. You access the 'how to' transform and enhance your life experiences positively and powerfully.

Celestial Healing brings you, super-awareness and super-energy to change your story should you wish to do so. It is here you can live more spectacularly and more peacefully whatever you experience. The magnificent Self steps forward to learn and undertake the deepest wisdom and learning in every life experience.

Your unique life is designed to bring powerful opportunities of living and loving as a better human being if you decide to do so.

I hope this book helps you greatly in this respect.

Blessings,
Tracey Ash, 2015

BOOK ONE

• • •

Life's most persistent and
urgent question is,
'What are you doing for others?'
— *MARTIN LUTHER KING, JR.*

Introduction

Since 1999, I have worked with and inspired change-makers, spiritual warriors and conscious individuals. This is a sweeping movement of individuals who love and dream of positive change for the turbulent times we live in now. These individuals are aware of the critical need for positive change in our world and communities and at the same time, are battling outdated, limiting stories that impede quality of life, human value and greater contribution.

This theme is visible in parents, passionate about changing history and world for the children they love. This theme is equally present in political activists and influencers who drive change in the charitable sectors, spirituality, science, education, work place, media and movie industries.

Valley of Kings, Modern Thebes, 2012.

No individual is more important in this exciting new frontier of conscious change where the outdated can be deconstructed. This theme is not necessarily new but the number of individuals is increasing rapidly as world events push change.

There is a new high-frequency template for mission and purpose available in unsurpassed freedom and intelligence, yet absolutely positive and good. This new template continuously refreshes and upgrades. This unlocks more and more of The Source Codes in a new super-template of awareness, transformation and manifestation potentials. It is rich in resource, effective and yet powerfully peaceful and evolutionary.

Is there a choice of 'opting in' to more stories of positive and good and 'opting out' of those deliberately slowing and destructive belief systems and structures? Absolutely yes! Since childhood, I have engaged in journeys of questioning, investigating, unravelling, travelling and listening for the stories that really matter in a quest to understand the purpose and value of our existence.

This is a journey exploring the stories of deeper understanding and wisdom in the lives we choose to create. These are the stories that deeply heal and free us whatever we experience. I adopted a meticulous strategy of awareness to engage and learn from every individual and experience, ancient monument and earth power site.

Deep below the surface is an encryption of truth within everything that exists or is being played out. It is this truth I listen for. It is this truth, I teach others to listen for. It is this truth that enriches life, value and meaning. I engaged in researching the best of meditation technologies and practices for self-discovery, transformation and manifestation. The more I listened, the more I learned how to transform, create and accelerate. I had found the key.

But this was not enough and I knew The Source Codes were for sharing, wherever I travelled to in the world. I kept discovering the keys over and over again. The keys are for teaching the path of the hero, awake, aware and vibrantly alive. The keys are for a magnificent new frontier of high-frequency living.

I absolutely love discovering and creating solutions for a better self and world today. This super-fascinates me. So how in a world of so many low-frequency destructive stories do we unlock and uphold a visible, magnificent self? This story is a familiar one; when you dip into a moment of powerful reflection or meditation, you may glimpse the magnificent self.

How do you hold onto it? That magnificence can make the world a better place and powerfully impact the lives of others, positively. This is the true path of the hero and healer. How do we as individuals ignite to listen through all the stories, to the most magnificent story of positive and good? How do we find this, trust and maintain this when there are so many other stories that distract? How do we easily learn how to power up and remain powered up where it matters in life? This is where we need to stay awake!

I decided that I would commit passionately to my work and mission with any honest individual who showed up requesting a better self and world. Excellent, high-frequency transformation and awareness technologies were developed to hit the important neutral point and the gateway into the magnificent self. This is the super-accelerator for human potential!

I have known how to meditate since childhood. This knowledge was inbuilt. Since 1987, I have trained in schools of Tibetan Buddhism, Zen Buddhism, Shinto, Yoga, Transcendental Meditation, Visual Entrainment, Western Meditation Technologies, Visualization and Positive Thinking, Shamanism, Subtle Energy Healing, Traditional Mediumship, Trance Channelling and Lucid Dreaming.

I am trained to see, vision, design and forecast. I hold a BA in Fashion Design. I have experienced vast ranges and quality of teaching. Original concepts are magnificent but this can gradually filter as a whisper of second-hand information. The power of high-frequency magnificence is untapped. The magic of transformation can be lost. Magnificence is often not known or upheld as critical by every teacher or facilitator.

Magnificence is the high-frequency switch that allows every individual the choice to leave toxic stories behind. Without this level of awareness, toxic stories are forever handed on. Often teachers and facilitators place heavy emphasis upon process and less upon consciousness excellence to accelerate miracles of transformation and awakening. *THIS IS A BIG MISTAKE!*

This can take you into dubious transformation where limiting stories frame and impede. This is not the way to truly facilitate and free another human being. This is also not the way to serve our future generations, our families, friends and clients. This is often wasted precious time spent for the student or seeker and can impede natural transformation and awakening processes if the teacher or facilitator is asleep. This story is handed down and duplicated.

My vision for individuals is not to power up in surprise, infrequent moments, or secret inner-world experiences but power up and unlock where it matters, the magnificence in precious life. *Making stories matter in life.* It is critical at this time, that miracles of transformation and manifestation can be part of our daily lives. Miracles are now required to free individuals to love and heal humanity and world.

Transformation and awakening processes now need to truly deliver, enhance and accelerate groundbreaking freedom and progress. We are running out of time. Engaging with the urgency of precious time and value of life force to create groundbreaking positive change is critical. Every individual experiencing repeated pain and suffering knows this. Humanity knows this but doesn't know how to unlock from the toxic cycles that are handed down and duplicated. This is the low-frequency conspiracy designed to slow evolution and manipulate and control.

I began learning how to engage with The Source Codes for manifesting positive life journeys and magical experiences that accelerate magnificence. Part of this ongoing research is with an elite group of scientists, PSI Scientific Institute Japan, investigating The Source Codes and what The Source Codes can bring to living miracles and excellence every day.

My research began with 'how to be' more magnificent every day and 'how to' transform redundant unhealthy low-frequency stories:

- How can we learn to super-improve listening, awareness and freedom in the important stories?
- How can we improve listening for those life-changing truths including purpose? After all, life-changing truths arrive in the neutral point sometimes immediately, sometimes miraculously, sometimes post-long, inner-conflict. The neutral point is essential for mission, health, awareness and well-being excellence. Unresolved trauma and conflict brings with it huge mop up operations. This limits what could be a new reality of health and human potential excellence. This limits what good can be achieved in the world.
- How can we increase precious time in high frequency? How could an individual super-magnify the magnificent self? How could an individual live more intelligently and powerfully in all the many stories every day?
- My journeys with thousands of individuals worldwide are based in high frequency, simple, solid foundations of inner-work and the important life work where it really matters. This cuts through the old and redundant unhealthy stories. This bends time and yet delivers change of dreams.
- How can we move from a place of knowing positive and good and living it? How do we maintain all-important high frequency for meticulous awareness and responsibility in as much of life as possible?

- The magnificent self is the new sovereignty of positive and good world change. Awareness changes lives and worlds. Usually, eventually and slowly. But what happens if we could speed up transformation and awareness?

High frequency reinforces magnificent self in the reality of so many stories. Life is always many stories, but magnificent self powers self to love to know what is worth giving precious time and life force to. High frequency brings groundbreaking intelligent choices, responsibility and action that changes your life and world.

Despite some time constraints, I began writing. Despite family life and my schedule of journeys with individuals, my schools and ancient power locations, I wrote this book to share groundbreaking knowledge with conscious individuals, positive change-influencers and spiritual warriors to live magnificent change.

By living in high frequency, super-awareness brings intelligent choices that are powerfully responsible and deeply healing not only to the self but to those you reach daily. In this self-care, your resource is your magnificent self. High frequency brings priceless freedom and it also brings this miracle to others. No more toxic stories. Challenges are no longer difficult and time-consuming. Inspiration and solutions ignite at your fingertips to transform life. Time bends and life journeys are miraculously enhanced. Raising the bar of excellence, little by little, by living more in The Source Codes as magnificent self.

This is living as a magnificent change-maker, knowing how to be free whatever the stories of the past, to deeply love and heal self, your precious time and life. You are peaceful; living peace ignites peace and awareness in the world you exist in. This is truly positive change.

With high frequency unlocked, stories can be easily evolved and modified to free incredible possibilities. Your life unlocks. High-frequency technologies ditch lengthy processes of time consuming conflict, resolution and hard work to freedom. This is The Source Codes switch. High frequency delivers outstanding, super-accelerated transformation results, repeatedly.

During journeys at ancient sites, the door opened and I entered The Source Codes. During journeys with individuals I unlocked The Source Codes in locating the stories of magnificence and truth. I could travel in time to honor the unique journey and purpose of each individual's life vision.

The Source Codes re-wires and enhances intelligence, peace, transformation and manifestation possibilities.

This brings a high-frequency sovereignty of choice, 'opting in' to positive and good cycles and 'opting out' of overtime in toxic cycles. This is essential life force maintenance. The Source Codes provide power reboot to upscale your awareness. The Sources Codes deliver on the urgent, daily and lifetime high-frequency transformation goals when changing stories is so urgent for those we love and care deeply about, the future of humanity and earth.

The Source Codes can deliver urgent world peace and positive action whether we work individually or generate in bigger world peace groups. Individual change is the key to greater global change.

To The Arab Spring, Egypt 2011

'I am a shining one clothed in power, mightier than any shining ones.'

— *THE EGYPTIAN BOOK OF THE DEAD*

On 21 March 2011, Spring Equinox, sixteen minutes of live, moving energy orbs and inter-dimensional Source Codes communication and realities footage was filmed at The Mortuary Temple of Rameses III, Egypt during my Return to Light Tour. Here is a renowned archaic power site and spectacular ancient monument close to the Valleys of the Queens and Kings.

This ancient monument is one of many sites visited in Egypt during my Return to Light Tours and ongoing investigations on what ancient monuments hold. A copy of the original film and subsequent research paper was donated to PSI Science Institute Japan and College of Psychic Studies, London. Former-President of College of Psychic Studies, Max Eames, described it as the best evidence he had seen.

The College of Psychic Studies has a unique archive library of world-class research collated since 1887. At The Mortuary Temple of Rameses III c.1180 BC, on the West Bank, Modern Luxor, a fascinating story of individual, planetary and humanity healing unfolded and was recorded live, during filming the tour experiences.

We had walked through the Valley of the Kings in the timeless Theban Hills noting the natural pyramid on the highest peak, and visited the tomb of Tutankhamen, at sunrise. Now, at The Mortuary Temple of Rameses III, the guardians of the monument ushered us through a labyrinth of shrines, into the Holy of Holies, out of sight.

In March 2011, it was a monumental time and a beginning of a cycle of unprecedented and accelerated world change, during The Arab Spring events and just days after Fukushima's world-changing nuclear disaster, post-tsunami.

This film recorded a live inter-dimensional narrative and stream of manifestations of feathers defying gravity and thousands of active energy orbs varying in speed and intensity (of varied size and shape–circular, circular with tails and colours; white, pink and blue). The group experienced together an unsurpassed super-transformation of life changing possibilities. This experience became a gateway template for work with individuals from all walks of life and the gateway template opened powerfully in various capitals around the globe.

At noon on 21 March 2011 as the four day Return to Light Tour came to a close, the group experienced the unprecedented super-power of the ancient Egyptian neteru, the power of Source Codes, as in ancient times.

The power of The Source codes re-wired back into consciousness. A continuous explosion of timeless ancient wisdom in thousands of multi-orbs activity of white, blue, green, perfect energy spheres, orbs with tails that culminated in a deep, rich, thick blanket of visible, opaque, white light, on the floor of the temple. These are the transformation experiences we dream of. And we filmed it.

White feathers were produced repeatedly from gateways defying gravity and being absorbed back at higher points as we brilliantly meditated and transformed in mission for greater world peace and healing. *The Egyptian Book of the Dead* depicts the weighing of the human heart on the Pillar of Judgement against the feather represented by Maat. Eternity is guaranteed when the feather and heart counterbalance.

Here, the pillar is surmounted by Thoth, Maat or Annubis and the feather is often exchanged for Maat herself. Maat or Annubis weigh the heart for entry to eternity. In this mortuary temple, the scene on the back wall depicts the Pillar of Judgement.

As I reviewed the film, as the mini-bus convoy transported us back to the east bank of Luxor, I was silent. The material was magnificent. The ancient wisdom was active. I had been meditating all my life but this was new, and more powerfully transformational and awakening, tangible and visible.

As I looked around at the group, every individual was vibrantly radiant and alive. Shining. The Source Codes, this super-speed technology had magically transformed the most important low-frequency stories – those big stories that corrupt our radiance. These are the stories designed for stealing our time, awareness, health, sovereignty and magnificence. These are the stories designed to steal away our energy for action for greater change and drop out of survival and control.

This list goes on. Could the most important dreams of freedom be unlocked? Could I have discovered The Source Codes switch that could outperform even the biggest, recurring, challenging stories that keep your magnificence a secret in life? Could superb possibilities be opened? Could this super-energy and super-time resource redefine patterns and cycles in life?

The Source Codes switch had fired a retuned, upgraded individual vision and health brilliance. Internal possibilities were opened and re-framed brilliantly again and again. With The Source Codes switched on, an individual is free. This individual has sovereignty, purpose and visible energy brilliance. Without this source Codes switch on, *TRANSFORMATION AND AWARENESS WITHOUT HIGH FREQUENCY EXCELLENCE BRINGS SO LITTLE LASTING FREEDOM AND ESSENTIAL BREAKTHROUGHS IN LIFE.* This keeps you stuck in irritating repeat cycles that locks you to low-frequency living.

So I had found the key to a door that could maintain transformation and magnificence in a massive, unlimited energy resource. Not any gateway – The Source Codes gateway to super-consciousness wiring for living every day.

But this wasn't only about healing the individual. This was about being free to be able to work together towards a global vision of world peace, world healing and service to humanity. This was about shifting obstacles, transforming old energies and often the excuses we choose to create. It became a gateway template for work with individuals from all walks of life. This template opened powerfully in various capitals and power sites around the globe as invitations manifest.

I became aware of the importance of this new frontier and global bond of individuals and communities, working to increase critical positive world change and healing despite challenging events. This was about remaining aware of critical world change events and using ancient technologies to lock into The Source Codes to stabilize more individual and collective peace, power and healing. *The starting point is simply self.*

I had been all too aware that the conscious individual requires gutsy yet peace-based action to achieve any level of decent contribution during these urgent times. *This would take more than positive thinking, vision boards and dream work.*

The law of attraction and manifestation approaches needed to be re-visited as world change defined positive and negative pathways for humanity. Navigating and choice would only happen in high frequency. There is little room for too many dips. High frequency becomes super-effective in The Source Codes.

This is vital for real freedom, contribution and action. Unresolved pain is no longer highest priority, peace is yours and your life force is unlocked for positive, powerful contribution at bigger picture levels. The Source Codes switch turns on your bigger life force and bigger magnificence. Agendas change and greater awareness ignites.

Could more powerful possibilities be created with each individual super-transformed? Yes! Big, challenging stories finally resolving and opening new ways and solutions. But could bigger super-miracles take place? Yes! Here, in this zone I held the key of super-transformation where one could magnificently exist in all stories, even the big, challenging stories that devour life force.

Could this sovereignty in every positive individual and community make a difference amidst world change crisis? I had always held this bigger vision but now the 'how to' was unfolding fast. Holding on to this zone was about to get so much more important as world change crisis accelerated; the key to a priceless inner resource. I was holding it and I so wanted to share it.

And I could, the invitations kept calling me to kick-start high-frequency individuals and communities and then into the bigger picture of planetary healing.

With very few tourists during The Arab Spring events of 2011, the Ancient Egyptian monuments instantly transformed into soothing landscapes of divine peace. Each individual on my Return to Light Tour made a powerful decision to travel against foreign office advice to create the groundbreaking positive change-maker. This important decision would awaken a new frontier of purpose and change-maker within each one of us.

My journey super-accelerated sharing new frontiers of 'how to' transform and awaken change-makers all over the world. With The Source Codes, I gained entry into a priceless sovereignty of high-frequency freedom and synchronicities, activating super-energy for action, manifestation and knowledge. I found myself at earth power sites all around the world communicating with powerful ancient wisdom encryption.

The ancients had left this timeless wisdom to help us know and shape our future. Here, the power of The Source Codes began to awaken visions of planetary evolution and healing. The Source Codes could unlock high-frequency paths of a divine and conscious humanity. The knowledge of ancient past was unlocking fast. Positive and good, ignited more of the Source Codes for powering my purpose and mission. Positive and good, could ignite more of the Source Codes in the purpose and mission of every individual I worked with.

I delivered the information on high-frequency life vision and manifestation and yet it was also their responsibility to uphold high-frequency life vision. This was the key to not only lasting individual peace but effective world peace and positive change acceleration.

I began asking what was happening in this groundbreaking Source Codes experience. What did The Source Codes experience do? What was being hard-wired back into consciousness? What did this signify for bigger picture possibilities, bigger purpose possibilities, bigger change possibilities, bigger potential possibilities? What did engaging in The Source Codes signify for transformation and awareness?

Were we entering a new frontier of high-frequency super-transformation that could be accelerated by simply, peacefully and lovingly choosing it? How could The Source Codes technologies be applied to increase groundbreaking human potential, world peace and positive change? What was the significance of ancient monuments and ancient power sites? Were there any other factors that would accelerate change this big? Astrological cycles? World events? Can any individual experience this? How do The Source Codes over-write deliberately low-frequency toxic stories?

The twenty-first century holds the possibility for an incredible new story for humanity. *NEW DIVINE TEMPLATES*. My question is how do we begin to successfully achieve this with each individual? Humanity can now go beyond repeated pain cycle focus, individually and globally, to enter a new frontier that builds foundations of positive change for our future generations.

The Source Codes can hard-wire new super-energy codes back into life, freeing us from prisons of outdated thinking, elite structures and limiting worlds in favour of better, conscious choices. High-frequency new stories can then be woven into future generations and the world, bending time and manifesting new possibilities for human potential, health and well-being excellence.

Celestial Healing tackles knowledge of our vast human potential versus the practical 'how to' on maintaining incredible healing, freedom, potential and manifestation every day. Going beyond the 'transformation breakthrough' roller coaster and intense 'ups and downs' to create a lifetime of greater magnificence.

The Source Codes turns up the energy resource volume when we really need it now – *TO BE ABLE TO CHOOSE THE TEMPLATES OF MAGNIFICENT MAN AND CREATE MAGNIFICENT DESTINY. THE SOURCE CODES IS THE POWER OF POSSIBLITIES, THE POWER TO LET GO, SURRENDER AND MANIFEST THE MOST MAGNIFICENT STORIES AND DREAMS.* This is the resource that allows you to flow in life's challenges, become more resilient, while experiencing all the stories of life, both good and bad.

The Source Codes Templates are *THE HIGH FREQUENCY VISIONARY, HEALER, PEACE-MAKER, CHANGE-MAKER*. To be even more specific, these templates ignite new transformational, awareness and manifestation possibilities. Solid, powerful, peaceful – this is no soft spiritual option, bringing the power of spirituality transformation and meditation right back into individual and life.

In the new template, individuals can live as positive change, awake and conscious of the journey of awakening that allows opting out of limiting and toxic stories.

A new template of resource and light returns to the individual igniting health and well-being excellence that equips and strengthens in a changing modern world where outdated and evolutionary co-exist. The challenges are overcome once you transform in the new templates.

These templates will maintain your groundbreaking energy levels, facilitating transformation and awareness breakthrough and manifestation miracles in life.

This is an entirely new frontier, deepening peace and power simultaneously. Deepening intelligent awareness and action for positive world change. You re-build up from outdated stories, your freedom is everyone else's. Here, you are the radiant warrior of peace, the positive change-maker, the hero, the peace-maker, the conscious visionary – making the real difference in the life you live.

I am passionate about sharing *THE SOURCE CODES* and a new journey of freedom that changes stories and lives. I love the people I work with. These are the people, just like you, who deeply care about the power of magnificent self and world change.

Temple of Seti I, Abydos, 2014.

CHAPTER 1

The Great Pyramids
of Ancient Egypt

'Before that we find the entity was in the Atlantean land, during those periods when there was the knowledge - through the teachers or leaders in the Law of One - as related to the destruction of the Atlantean or Poseidon land.

And the entity was among those who journeyed from Atlantis or Poseidia itself, first to the Pyrenees or Portugese land and later into what would be called in the present the Egyptian land - during those periods after the recall of Ra-Ta, when he with Saneid and the activities from the land of On and Oz and those from what is now known as the Gobi land attempted to make for a unification of the knowledge.

Hence we find the entity then, Ax-Ten-tna, as would be said in the present, was the first to set the records that are yet to be discovered, or yet to be had of those activities in the Atlantean land, and for the preservation of the data, that as yet to be found from the chambers of the way between the sphinx and the pyramid of records.

Hence is it a wonder in the present that the entity is in this experience under the symbol and the sign of both the sphinx and the pyramid, when there is to be given a new awakening in many portions of the earth?

The activities of the entity then had much to do not only with the historic reaction but the developments for individual activities of groups, as the classifications came, were the ORDER of the entity as related to the King, as related to the Priest, and those that were sent or came as emissaries or teachers or representatives of those tenets that were gathered during that experience in the Egyptian land.'

—*'EDGAR CAYCE on Atlantis,'*

Edgar Evans Cayce, (1486-1, 27-31; Nov. 26, 1937)

The Great Pyramids, Giza. *Tracey Ash 2013.*

2012, Journey

At Giza, Cosmos and Earth are held as one –heart of ancient earth held in heart of sacred cosmos. Heart of humanity anchored at heart of sacred cosmos. Earth, humanity and cosmos converging, emerging and radiating at this spectacular ancient monument and earth power site.

The Great Pyramids and Sphinx hang from the cosmos, anchored spectacularly in the granite below. Forbidding cosmic generators, cosmic monuments recording infinite knowledge of man and humanity beyond time and the limiting stories we hold world in. The site at Giza is a monumental centre of divinity beyond any words. A key for change.

I ignite in quantum initiations in the Great Hall of Knowledge that reveals to those who see in time and beyond time. Giza is the world's sacred epicentre.

I vision The Path of the Initiate, a profound and unstoppable calling. At Giza, truths unfold in every experience. Truths awaken transformation in billions of potent miracles. These truths are many forms of me. Giza draws the magic of eternity and divinity closer. I merge. Within many moments, many hours of awakening, I am eternity and divinity. My visit at Giza lasts more than eight hours. This is during my Return to Light Tour.

In the second pyramid, Khafra, the Divine awakens me. As I lie in the deep velvet granite of the sarcophagus in the vast chamber, in the darkness, I become peace. I become one, in time and out of time, I flow, I transform. Afterwards, I sit square to the sarcophagus where I acknowledge the eternity of the divine feminine as I view this momentary world. She views the world through me, touching me. I see clearly and deeply the six people also present in this chamber. There are many moments with this divinity – knowing she is me.

Illusions and distractions melt away. The divine feminine holds sacred, eternal peace, in older eternal knowledge beyond words. All else is fractional time and knowledge. It matters only that I become her, that I know her a little more.

On the wall, two great images of archangels Michael and Gabriel manifest over seconds. The chamber is filled with intense energies that transform me. In every second, I am more awake. I bathe in celestial silence. I ponder how the world could be if we could glimpse this magnificence.

I walk Giza, as the ancients before me, barefoot in the searing sun of the afternoon. I avoid the modern world distractions, the throng of tourists in feisty sales pitches. I live in eight hours of divinity, aware of many lives I have walked here. I experience my destiny. I ponder over the meaning of existence, and of true divinity, positively shaping world for all time.

This vision is so immense that illusion will always melt no matter what is played out. During this initiation of November 2012, I am awakened for all eternity, knowing that humanity will awaken from its current sleep. I am reminded of the speed of world change and that greater love and wisdom is present where peace is found.

This is the miracle of Giza mirroring what we could be – if we could glimpse it. This magnificence would change world and humanity forever. Our Divinity would be known as a majestic, infinite and loving intelligence shaping our destiny and future.

In Khufu, The King's Chamber and Grand Gallery is stark, vast and monumental. The Great Pyramid is the divine temple of sacred union. Michelangelo's Creation of Adam is manifest before me in the great cosmic mirror of the granite walls that have recorded humanity and time. Christ is the vision held in my heart. Silence intensifies. The fire of peace intensifies. A profound and infinite peace. There are no limitations, no end, no beginning.

I experience timelessness. It is only my breath that keeps bringing me to the moment in which I exist. I could surrender forever at this iconic site. This is an incredible power site, a gateway to the template of Christ, a cosmic and divine knowledge that can only be experienced. This is an eternal knowledge revealed through many initiations revealing secrets for world change today.

Pyramid Science

The Great Pyramids of Ancient Egypt were designed to hardwire and amplify power of divinity and universe within individual and world. This is the path of initiate and pharaoh. Today, Giza is still a global epicenter of an infinite wisdom seed of humanity.

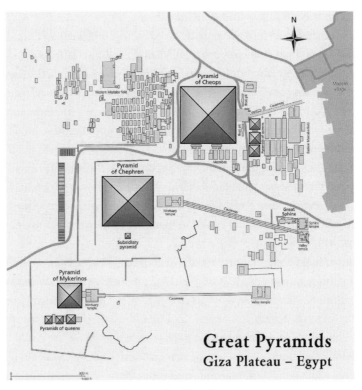

Necropolis, Giza, Egypt.

The Great Pyramid complex is designed as sacred architecture and technologies for magnificent stories of transformation for humanity and earth. How and why? The Great Pyramid alone is truly awesome – its height is 481.9349 feet, its base covers 13.1 acres, it weighs in at 6 million tonnes, built in an estimated 2.3 million individual blocks, and once covered by 115,000 brilliant white limestone casing stones, with tolerances of 1/100 inch – were confirmed by archaeologist and surveyor, Sir William Mathews Flinders Petrie (3 June 1853 – 28 July 1942).

The brilliant white limestone casing is alabaster or limestone calcite originated as liquid, ANKH UAS is 'sap of life' and ANKH is 'life'. Alabaster is white pure or clear. Calcite alabaster is found as a stalagmite deposit, from limestone caverns connected with archaic ritual, or travertine in springs of calcareous water. Its most famous place of origin in ancient Egypt is HAT-NUB or 'house of gold'. HAT-NUB is located twenty kilometers southeast of Tel el-Amarna.

This information connects us with The Hermetic Opus. Hat-nub is chamber or house of gold. Hat-nub is the sarcophagus chamber in tombs, the workshops where statues of the neteru were created and the place in the Serapeum where the statue of Osiris was placed. Osiris encapsulates eternity. Our eternity is known through alchemy.

Alchemy transforms frequency, unlocking time, vision and reality. The monuments at Giza demonstrate advanced technologies, facts that are spectacular even to modern conventional minds. According to Mark Lehner, Director of the Giza Plateau Mapping Project, its height is 481 feet or 146.59 metres, this gives 1460 or 1461 years that correlate with the Sothic calendar (or Sirius star system). 51°50°40 yields the decimal number 25.9222222: this is the Platonic cycle of 25,920 years.

As we now move into the next world phase, into the next 25,920 years cycle, the new template of humanity ignites rebirth and resurrection. The ancients encoded this ancient information at Giza. The next evolutionary phase of humanity blows open elite power structures. Ancient Egypt is critical in understanding the next phase of world change. Ancient Egypt holds missing information key in our evolution.

The north face is aligned to almost perfect true north. The east face is aligned to almost perfect east. Both, the west face and south face are exactly aligned true west and true south. The north side is 755 feet, 8.9818 inches. The west side is 755 feet, 9.1551 inches. The east side is 755 feet, 10.4937 inches. The south side is 756 feet, 0.9739 inches. Perfect north, south, east and west, the cardinal directions are utilized in shamanic processes of visioning and time travel. But there is more that has been found.

The Great Pyramid measurements contain the earth's size, the length of one year, the distance from the earth to the sun, star alignments and the precession of the equinoxes, the cycle of 25, 920 years. This is mind-blowing information for world change now!

- The Equinox Precession cycle is 25,920 years.
- A new constellation appears on the horizon every 2160 years.
- 25,920 years is one 360° rotation or cycle.
- Each constellation is 2160 years. Each 2160 years or 30° represents a new constellation or sign.

- 12; 30; 72; 360; 2160; 4320; 25,920 are all precessionary numbers.
- Leo is 10,800-8640 BC, Cancer is 8640-6480 BC, Gemini is 6480-4320 BC, Taurus is 4320-2160 BC, Aries is 2160 BC-0, Pisces is 0-2160 AD, Aquarius is 2160-4320 AD.
- 25.92 x 2=51.84. The decimal number 51.84 expresses 51°50°24. This is the angle of the apex of The Great Pyramid.

Pyramid research by the Russian National Academy of Sciences that includes the Russian Academy of Medical Sciences, Institute of Theoretical and Experimental Biophysics, Graphite Scientific Research Institute, and the Institute of Physics in Ukraine, discovered some of the following fascinating scientific results produced in pyramid structures:

- *The immune system of organisms increased upon in the pyramid. The Leukocyte composition of the blood increased. Also increased regeneration of tissues.*
- *Agricultural seeds placed in a pyramid for 1-5 days showed a 30-100% increase in yield.*
- *A Russian Military radar located an energy column rising several miles high in the sky above the 22m high Lake Seliger pyramid. Several months after this pyramid was built, the Ozone layer improved in the atmosphere in Russia.*
- *Areas near the pyramids appear to diminish seismic activity. Instead of one large powerful earthquake occurring, there are hundreds of tiny ones. Also violent weather appears to decrease in the area surrounding the pyramids.*
- *A pyramid complex was built in an oil field in Southern Russia at Bashkiria. The oil became less viscous by 30% and the yield of oil increased. These results were confirmed by Gubkin, Moscow, Academy of Oil and Gas.*
- *Newborns were given solutions that had been placed in the pyramid and their health increased.*
- *Experiments with about 5,000 people in jails in Russia showed that after a few months most crimes almost disappeared and behaviour improved. This was attributed to the salt and pepper added to their food. The salt and pepper had been placed in the pyramid.*
- *The potency of pharmaceuticals increased with decreasing side effects after being placed in the pyramid.*

- *There is an increase in survival of cellular tissue infected by viruses and bacteria. The pyramid decreases the strength of viruses and bacteria.*
- *When radioactive waste is placed inside the pyramid, decreased levels of radioactivity are recorded.*
- *Changes in superconductivity temperature thresholds and properties of semiconductors and carbon materials after being placed in a pyramid.*
- *Ordinary water does not freeze even at 40 degrees below zero and retains its properties for years after being placed in a pyramid.*
- *Synthesized diamonds become harder and purer after being placed in a pyramid. The possible reason behind the super-precision machining techniques at Giza, that outstrip even technologies today.*

36,632 Years Before the First Dynasty

Here is fascinating information on pre-dynastic history indicating that there are 36,632 years, forgotten or omitted before the First Dynasty of Pharaoh Menes (Akha) c.3218–3035.

- Could it be the pyramids also belong to an earlier period of forgotten knowledge?
- Pharaoh Akha is an important deliberate clue linked visibly with Akhu, an archaic template of cosmic man found in royal lineage. Akha is importantly recorded as Hor-Aha, a further reference to Hor (Horus) linking with Christ.

This template will be explored in many other connections that myriad-link a new template of humanity. But where are these forgotten stories found?

In *Sacred Science, the King of Pharaonic Theocracy*, R.A. Schwaller de Lubicz writing about the Royal Papyrus of Turin, says that it stated a complete list of kings from Menes to the New Empire. The first columns of this document though showed the even earlier reigns, those preceding Menes.

From remaining fragments of The Royal Papyrus of Turin, evidence points to a vast, missing history.

> '...*venerables Shemsu-Hor, 13,420 years.*
> *Reigns up to Shemsu-Hor, 23,200 years.*
> *(total 36,632)*
> *(to) King Menes (Akha)...*'

- The first column of The Royal Papyrus of Turin is a list of ten neteru, each name inscribed inside a significant royal cartouche, depicting royal lineage, another important clue. This list includes The Great Ennead, Ptah, Ra, Shu, Geb, Osiris, Seth, Thoth, Maat and Horus during Zep Tepi or First Time. The Creation Myth of The Great Ennead of Heliopolis, also links us with The Shining Ones. Later explored.
- The second column is a king list before First Dynasty Menes (Akha).
- The remaining fragments establish nine dynasties and the Shemsu-Hor. The Shemsu-Hor are the Followers of Horus and direct lineage of Pharaonic Ancient Egypt. The archaic Horus connects us with Akhu, the cosmic template of man and also to the first pharaoh, Menes, Akha or Hor-Aha and subsequent dynasties. This is important information.

Diodorus of Sicily, in *Bibliotheca Historica*, reports, between 60-30 BC, chronicles of deities and heroes in Ancient Egypt for 18,000 years and kings for 15,000 years giving 33,000 years of history in total. Manetho, 3rd century BC, estimates a history that spans 24,927 years, 15,150 years of divine dynasties and 9777 years to dynasties of kings. George Syncellus d. 810, who was a Byzantine chronicler and ecclesiastic scholar, concludes that thirty royal dynasties are preceded by twenty-five divine dynasties, each of a Sothic cycle of 1461 years.

This span of divine dynasties is a massive 36,525 years and has been disregarded by orthodox chronology, classified as myth. On the account of Herodotus in the fifth century BC, conventional Egyptology has accepted Khufu (Cheops), Khafre (Chephren) and Menkaure (Mycerinus) as the pyramid-builders of the Fourth Dynasty. His account has been absorbed without question.

In Chapter Two I explore further how The Source Codes designs are anchored at The Great Pyramid.

CHAPTER 2

Source Codes Designs

The male as animus and female as anima encompass a spectrum of positive and negative opposites that ascend or progress through pyramid structure to the zero point. The zero point is depicted as the apex of the triangle or pyramid; only at this gateway, polarities are neutralized and can be fused with The Source Codes or Zero Point field.

In Alchemy's Magnus Opus, the Conjuctio is the unification of masculine and feminine into a perfect unbreakable circle. It is The Great Work, and an alchemical term for the process of creating the philosopher's stone.

- The philosopher's stone was the central symbol of the mystical terminology of alchemy, symbolizing perfection and finest, enlightenment. It was believed to be an elixir of life, for rejuvenation and achieving immortality. The circle is depicted as the solar disc and can be traced to Ra and The Shining Ones.
- The circle is the archaic source of Ra. Ra is documented as highest divine power. Ra links divinity and alchemy, and is known to produce the most secret liquid or elixir of eternal youth. Ra placed the serpent in chains and personified individuals who could control the primordial energy of the cosmos embodied in the serpent, known as The Shining Ones of the Garden of Eden, Southern Lebanon before 8,000 BC.

I discovered the simple drawing of the solar disc of Ra above a pyramid on the wall of a hidden chamber in tomb V62 of Tutankamon (earlier Tutankaton), in Valley of the Kings, Luxor. Tutankamon (ca. 1332 BC – 1323 BC, conventional Egyptology) and direct lineage to Akhenaton.

I experienced the same vision of a simple pyramid and solar disc whilst lying in meditation in the granite sarcophagus of the King's Chamber, in The Great Pyramid. The memories of a cosmic template of humanity are locked in our histories and DNA. Moved from its original position, the granite sarcophagus was originally aligned with the apex of The Great Pyramid, the gateway to The Source Codes. This is another clue in unlocking the purpose of The Great Pyramid.

Akhu is the cosmic template of man, the next template of humanity. At Giza, gravity anchors this template in sacred architecture. Entry to The Source Codes and this template is possible when the foundation energy centres in the human energy field are power activated. The energy system can be unlocked by following the design of The Great Pyramid.

This is a genius master key for positively influencing and manifesting the future. In alchemy traditions, the theme of red, white and black prevails and Giza is constructed to this theme. Red granite, white limestone and black granite have been selected with an intelligent vision of alchemy as gateway to our divinity.

Here is a purposeful clue for our design mastery of consciousness. The red as positive and the white as negative correspond to the etheric nerve channels or nadis in the Hindu physio-kundalini chakra system in the human body. The Nadi or channels are the Pingala, positive, male and red and the Ida, negative, female and white. These Nadi or channels cross at the zero point – the Shushumna.

The seven energy centres or chakras, along the human spine are where the two nadi–the Pingala and Ida–cross. The two nadis or channels are symbolized and represented by the two serpents of the Caduceus. The caduceus is the ancient symbol of ultimate healing. In Sanskrit 'kundalini' means circular. This is a symbolic bond and journey of inner knowledge and responsibility.

'It seems that this great glyph of antiquity, still in use throughout the world as a perennial emblem of the healing professions, had more arcane meanings. Revered in the days of Ancient Egypt as the Staff of Thoth, a magical rod crowned with the sun-disc, and encoded by two writhing serpents, it has come down to us through our succeeding cultures as a potent symbol of the Hermetic Arts.

Thoth had become Hermes, and later the Roman Mercury. Considering the mercurial nature of the terrestrial currents, which apparently flow like quicksilver through the surface of the earth, the conclusion seems inescapable – the serpent Wand derives its power from its symbolism of energies operating in balance, the basic energies of existence mutually interacting.

Mystics throughout the ages have seen the Caduceus as a representation of how the subtle energies of the human body function – the central staff in the Eastern tradition, the Shushumna, the pillar that has its physical counterpart in the spine and the enclosing channel of the central nervous system. Around this spiral is the twin energies symbolized as serpents, the Ida and Pingala, the former ruled by the moon, the latter the sun.

It is these powerful energies, which are stirred into activity when certain disciplines concentrate on the rising of the kundalini, the serpent power which starts at the base of the spine and rises upwards through the successive chakras, or subtle energy centres, to bring spiritual illumination.

If the earth is itself a vast being, understood by both ancient wisdom and the Gaia Theory of Modern Science, the Hermetic Principle, "as above, so below" should also apply to the living body of the planet.'

— *PAUL BROADHURST AND HAMISH MILLER*

The Sun and The Serpent

And this is what occurs in Ancient Egypt within cosmic architecture, architectural grids and the initiate! Gopi Krishna describes the kundalini force as the important evolutionary energy in man.

In Tantra and Yoga, translated as union, the kundalini process and the journey into the Zero Point Field allows consciousness to infinitely progress. This is also described as The Diamond Body or Rainbow Body. The Diamond Body or Rainbow Body, is of course, the Akhu. The secret domain of mystics.

The Zero Point - Source Codes

The chakras or energy centres correspond with seven levels of consciousness and the first seven levels of reality anchored into seven major portals in the body. The mastery of the seven levels of consciousness brings mastery of the first seven levels of reality.

Mastery of the seven levels of consciousness is an exact process of achieving the zero point at each nadi or chakra that connects deep within the body-mind. This manifests profound levels of awareness and transformation.

From foundation level, level one; only from this level can precise mastery be gained. Then access to the next level unlocked, level two, and so forth.

I suggest Giza was designed for processes of super-consciousness. I propose the architecture of the Great Pyramids complex was directed by a pre-Ancient Egyptian lineage directly connected with The Shining Ones. The primary builder is Osiris. The pre-cursor design to the pyramids at Giza is the Ziggurat of Nabu at Borsippa (Basipki), which was known as 'The House of the Seven Bonds of Heaven and Earth'. It represented the cosmic link between the earth and cosmos. James Fergusson, in *A History of Architecture in All Countries* (1893) wrote:

> '*This temple, as we know from the decipherment of the cylinders which were found on its angles, was dedicated to the seven planets or heavenly spheres, and we find it consequently adorned with the colours of each. The lower, which was also greatly panelled, was black, the colour of Saturn; the next, orange, the colour of Jupiter; the third red, emblematic of Mars; the fourth yellow, belonging to the Sun; the fifth and sixth green and blue respectively, as dedicated to Venus and Mercury; and the upper probably white, that being the colour belonging to the moon, whose place in the Chaldean system would be uppermost.*
>
> *The connection with Babylon is made by Berossus (c.3BC); he ascribed a total reign of 432,000 years (120 shar's of 3600 years) to the mystical kings who ruled before the flood. Here he describes 2160,000 years between creation and universal catastrophe. The Babylonian Kings are credited with incredible reigns, Alulim, of 28,000 years, Alagar of 36,000 years, Emnenluanna of 43,200 years, Emmengalanna of 28,800 years, Dumuzi, of 36,000 years, Ensipazianna of 21600 years and Uburtutu of 18,000. Note the link here with Osiris and Dumuzi.*'

The difficulty we have in decoding The Great Pyramid is that our consciousness is not currently advanced to straddle multi-connected, inter-dimensional levels of understanding. We may understand this concept but we do not know how to operate in it or as it. This is the big illusion when we read, believe and opt out of experience. These levels of understanding require mastery. Our current reality has been manipulated because of this critical knowledge. Mastery of seven levels of consciousness opens mastery of seven levels of reality, then entry to Source Codes. This opens the next seven levels of consciousness and reality.

The zero point can be described as the reality of resolution, united, neutralized or fully transformed. In transliminal experiences, states or phases such as in meditation or powerful reflection, the zero point enables us to see the deeper connections between consciousness and cycles of life. This is critical awareness and transformation accelerates manifestation. The zero point is very challenging to maintain everyday despite what is often promised in transformation or spirituality processes. Yet, this is critical for manifesting.

Positive experiences deliver a peak and negative experiences create a dip. The zero point is critical in every cycle, of life and death, of day and night, of breakdown and breakthrough. It was believed that during The Equinox, the exact zero point between two cycles, opens a portal or gateway between earth and cosmos through which Divinity radiates.

It is here, we can influence our reality and future. This is The Source Codes gateway. The gateway to magnificent manifestation.

The exact alignment of The Great Pyramid during Spring Equinox falls on 21/22 March and creates no shadow. This is the date on which we filmed The Source Codes in 2011 at The Mortuary Temple of Rameses III, Luxor.

Osiris is celebrated with The Spring Equinox connecting The Great Pyramid site with Christ and Osiris. Osiris connects us during this period with the similar Celtic Green Man, Roman Attis, Babylonian Tammuz and Sumerian Damuzi. Within The Great Pyramid architecture, Christ Consciousness becomes very exciting. This is our own story of rebirth.

Conscious Retreat Egypt, Great Pyramids Complex, Giza.

The ancient Egyptian word for pyramid is *PER NETER*, translated as 'house of the neteru'. During history, neter has been deliberately mistranslated or mistakenly translated as deity. If neter is a *SOURCE CODE template*, I suggest these are the essential, missing consciousness templates of humanity.

And what if Source Codes templates can be hardwired back into consciousness if we understand 'how'? *I propose this is the function of the Great Pyramids complex. I suggest the secrets of super-human consciousness technologies can be easily understood and entered.*

The zero point can also be described in sexual union and conception. Male and female unite and the child is the embodiment of the third force, the zero point. At the moment of conception the child or fertilized ovum is represented as the divine spark of creation. The child is the divine spark. We all are born divine. This is the common bond of humanity until our Source Codes resource is depleted through continuous bombardment of low-frequency limiting stories.

These low-frequency toxic stories play out in continuous toxic cycles and illusions. Often, we blindly accept these stories unaware that stories can be changed. Often, these stories are accepted consciously to serve agenda, pain and suffering. The Great Pyramids complex provides sacred architecture and technologies for the rebirth of magnificent stories and templates of humanity and earth.

Sirius

The next world phase unlocks deepest commitment to self-responsibility to create most magnificently in a world of many stories. There is no longer time to hold manipulation, blame and control in place as we accelerate into the next world phase. 25,920 years is the tipping point for miraculous transformation possibilities. You switch on awakening and responsibility as you ignite hero. This is the clue the ancients left and the power elite structures would continue to deny us. Awakening is about to get super-accelerated!

The story of Christ confirms that within each individual is a seed template of cosmic man. We know that the ancient Egyptians understood the Sirius Star System was connected to Isis, Hathor and Osiris, Horus. We also know that according to Mark Lehner, Director of the Giza Plateau Mapping Project, the height of The Great Pyramid is 481 feet or 146.59 meters. This gives 1460 or 1461 years correlating with the Sothic (Sirius) calendar. Isis is powerfully linked with Sirius. Isis is also very powerfully described,

'I am all that has been, that is, and that will be.'
— *THE TEMPLE OF ISIS, AT SAIS, ANCIENT EGYPT.*

If the Sirius Star System is a clue in the next template of humanity, then The Great Pyramids at Giza may also claim our celestial origins. The Sirius connection with Isis, Hathor, Osiris and Horus is profuse in Ancient Egyptian mythology.

- Sirius A is 1000 times brighter than Sirius B.
- Sirius A is 35.5 times the luminosity of our sun.
- Consider the relevance of this information in higher frequency templates of humanity that can super-power peace, evolution and world change.

In India, The Shining Ones are known as the Naga. In Mesoamerica, The Shining Ones are known as The Feathered Serpents. In China, the Shining Ones are known as The Water Beings. Could it be also The Great Pyramid site is the original birth-site of Christ Consciousness for every individual?

The cosmic template of humanity is found powerfully and visibly encoded in Giza more than at any other sacred or religious site worldwide.

Global deities symbolize the same bond of universal spiritual processes that are naturally played out in our life cycle and are accelerated, should we choose processes of transformation and awakening. The global network of pyramids also deserves further study – they contain deliberate clues, solutions and healing for now.

At Giza, The Source Codes process was designed to achieve highest levels of evolution – igniting the template of cosmic humanity in reproduction. This is seen in the progression of ancient Egyptian dynasties to Tutankamon who is the cosmic template of man, as were Akhenaton and Nefertiti.

The ancients recorded and predicted future cycles of humanity in precise tracking of cosmic cycles. I understand that this is encoded within the design of The Great Pyramid complex. Not all three pyramids are open simultaneously to the public. The Great Pyramid complex communicates a new template of humanity we need now, during critical world change.

Osiris, Isis and Horus templates correlate to the three major pyramids dedicated to Khufu, Khafre and Menkaure. Each pyramid acts as an evolutionary machine. Significant planetary and celestial alignment also creates powerful anchors for world peace and healing.

Peace is the finest response to challenging self and world events. We are heading on a journey together towards peace.

CHAPTER 3

My Ancient Memories of Abu Ghorab and the Museum of Cairo, March 2012

I walk through the Museum of Egyptian Antiquities, through the hall dedicated to the Amarna Period dated c. 1353-1356 BC and the Colossi of Akhenaton that continue to intrigue and fascinate generation after generation. I stop, breathe and absorb, reminding myself that the Colossi were only discovered in 1925. The Museum of Cairo was purpose built in 1902 and designed to hold some of the most magnificent Pharaonic Antiquities the world will ever see.

One hundred and seven halls, one hundred and sixty thousand objects, it is a sprawling chronological race through Ancient Egypt in neoclassical style and dusty Egyptology. It is unique and magnificent in grand British Colonial style and scale, indeed, one of the greatest antiquities museums in the world.

I am alone as I walk in silence through the avenue of exhibits. I experience a shockwave of energy that runs through me. I am startled by this immediacy and I suddenly stop. I turn one hundred and eighty degrees, to perfectly lock with an intricately carved double, limestone statue or dyad. The dyad is 80 cms high, intact colour and hieroglyphs, depicting Mery-Re, Mery-Aten or Mery-Neith with his wife Anuj, Anay and Aniuia. The inscription reads,

'scribe of the temple of Aten at Akhataten (and)
in Memphis, Meryre justified.'

I hurry towards it and note the luminous perfect crystal limestone forms of the male and female figures. Meryre, with his wife seated in perfect resonance and harmony. Immediately, I am dropped into an incredible connection. It is Meryre, exactly as I had drawn myself during past life recall in the mid-nineties. The synchronicities were startling; Akhenaton, Tel el Amarna, Abu Ghorab and Giza.

During the mid-nineties, I time-travelled myself into an Ancient Egyptian lifetime in Abu Ghorab. Here, I experienced myself as an Initiate of the Path of Light.

(My past life facilitator was utterly perplexed when I refused to experience any epic story immersed in pain and suffering. This took her and her session right 'out of the box' and her expected pain story, into an incredible lost ancient knowledge.)

Old school meeting new school, I careered into an incredible ancient world of cosmic healing super-technologies. Immediately and vividly, I could see myself as a male. Barefoot, tall and slim, almost luminous, palest blue grey eyes, long, thick, curl after curl of waist-length hair and a white, simply cut robe. I walked the path of the initiate, silently in knowledge of this unusual pyramid complex, of inter-connected flat roof pyramids.

I remembered it was my destiny to know how to manipulate cosmic technologies and high frequencies that could be stored in the earth's gravitational field. I remembered that it was my destiny to transform each individual who presented him-self or her-self silently for super-transformation processes. There was a large template anchored into the floor, a repeated geometric system of deep, white calcite basins fed by liquid light. The narrow slits in the pyramid template were purposefully designed to anchor the ancient light of stars and universe in gravity within meticulous site maps. Exact frequencies were sculpted and held as spheres in the calcite basins.

I had not yet visited Egypt. I was then in my twenties and my career had not unfolded yet. I was fascinated in meditation of course but this was science fiction crazy! Little did I know, this self would teach me everything, everything that I now know and will probably ever know about destiny, realities and consciousness.

These time travelling experiences have become more and more about my ancient past into my immediate future and the work I now do all over the world, unlocking the important stories, resetting consciousness, changing frequencies to align with stories for positive and greater good; the path that is light.

These experiences exposed exact technologies for re-setting high-frequency consciousness, to upscale purpose and destiny. At the Museum of Cairo in 2012, I careered again back into Ancient times, to Meryre. This double statue, was the exact image as I had sketched in the mid-nineties past-life replay. Double-checking all the details in front of me… tall, skinny limbed, barefoot, long, thick curled hair, simple white robe, exactly just as I had drawn all the details.

I had also drawn out a spectacular pyramid site and cosmic template for re-booting high-frequency consciousness and destiny. The cosmic template required immense energy resource, converging earth frequencies and cosmic sources held in advanced technology machined white calcite domes.

The statue of Meryneith or Meryre and his wife Anuy was found in the tomb of Meryneith, Saqqara, in 2011. Cairo Museum.

The temple of Aten is still yet undiscovered. Let us set the scene further. The statue of Meryneith (or Meryre) and his wife Anuy was discovered in the tomb of Meryneith, Saqqara, in 2011 by a joint expedition of the Leiden Museum of Antiquities and Leiden University. Meryneith or Meryre is described in inscriptions as 'Greatest of Seers of the Aten' (High Priest of Aten) and 'High Priest of the Temple of Neith'.

He is also known as 'Steward of the Aten'. Meryre ended his career under Tutankhamen as 'High Priest of Aten' at this Memphite temple after serving Akhenaton.

The Aten played a dominant role at Memphis before and after Akhenaton. Akhenaton did not solely focus the Cult of Aten at Amarna and it may be worthwhile reconsidering his importance at Thebes, Memphis and Amarna.

It may also be worth noting his connection with the cosmic template of man and initiation processes at Memphis. It is fascinating to note... this information is often deleted and corrupts the story of Akhenaton.

If we revisit this information, we begin to understand the importance of these sites and historical figures as incredible visionaries of divinity and humanity.

There is very little research available which is why I spend so much time researching these sites to discover the stories of truth about our ancient past.

Fast-forward to March 2013. By road the journey to Abu Ghorab's ancient monument is accessed through a bumpy dirt track into a pretty mango grove that leads onto the Sahara Desert trail. Often the Sahara winds blow hard, making just walking and visibility difficult. Abu Ghorab has no official ticket office and my Return to Light Tour group is led through the desert by those claiming to be guardians of the monument, for a fee.

After a moderate hike, we spill into an isolated, silent, ruinous landscape with the pyramid and temple complex still visible. In front of this impressive pyramid, now in great decline, is a spectacular crystal altar. I stop for a moment to absorb this site. With no official ticket office, we have time.

I begin meditating on the crystal altar or hotep – aligned perfectly to the cardinal directions – spoken word is not necessary; the other group members slide into the sacred silence and begin meditation. From here, Abu Sir pyramid complex is a short walk, both Saqqara and Giza, often visible. I prepare myself to work with each individual in each of the white calcite domes, the domes I had sketched out in the mid-nineties that depicted this temple complex.

At Abu Ghorab in 2013, there was something different. I instinctively knew the layout and found one of the domes still anchored in the floor of the temple complex. The other domes had been moved and nine, positioned to the east, still intact. I request the group to prepare for Celestial Healing. I allocate each individual a dome to sit or stand in. I diagnose and assess each individual's healing and destiny agendas. The resonance and alchemy of the group template is critical. Individual transformation begins, first re-setting frequency then opening new gateways of transformation.

It is an important appointment with destiny that moves me to tears. I am home.

Abu Ghorab is a Fifth Dynasty Egyptian pyramid and solar temple complex on the Saqqara plateau that links closely with Abu Sir (referenced as Old Kingdom, 2465-2323 BC in conventional Egyptology). It was last excavated between 1892 and 1901 by German scholars Borchardt, Schaeffer and von Bissing and later studied in the 1950s by the Swiss Institute directed by Ricke.

Abu Ghorab is also professed to be one of the oldest ceremonial sites in the world according to indigenous oracular traditions of Egypt (dating to before 5000 BC). Here, the neters arrived in physical form at this site. At this temple complex, fragments of scene reliefs depict the creation of the world by Ra. Here, the site of Abu Ghorab contains the Sun Temple of Ne-user-re.

In addition to his pyramid at Abu Sir, Niuserre built this Sun Temple 'Nekhen-Re' (Stronghold of Re) at Abu Ghorab with similar features to that of a typical pyramid complex. This solar temple had a Valley Temple portion connected by a causeway to an open court containing the main pyramid base structure topped by an obelisk and a separate white calcite altar, some six metres long.

The altar is machined with advanced technology to produce four precise hotep symbols encasing an exact sphere in the centre, depicting 'peace', 'offerings' and 'Re satisfied'. The obelisk is ib-re, symbolic as the 'heart of Ra'.

This Memphite complex can be further connected with the Benben Stone and the earlier archaic Heliopolitan Creation Myth. We will later explore more of the Abu Sir and Abu Ghorab archaic connection with Osiris and the Anunnaki. With further investigation, Nekhen-Re can also be connected with the deities, Nekhen and Neith. (Neith is an archaic cosmic template of divine female – weaving the fabric of the earth.)

Ancient Memphis was the capital of Ancient Egypt through much of the Pharaonic period, built at or near the head of the Nile Delta. According to Egyptian myths and classical legends, the first king, Menes or Aka, of Egypt established the city in c.3100 BC. Its ruins are located near the town of Mit Rahina, 20 km (or 12 miles) south of Modern Cairo.

Its location is close to the elite necropoleis and monumental architecture of Saqqara, Zawiyet, Abu Sir, Abu Ghorab, Aryan, Giza and Abu Rawash. Memphis brings the question of whether just one nucleated site existed, because Memphis shifted due to changing climatic conditions and the course of the Nile. It was the three way portal between Europe, Asia and Africa for trade and disseminating far-reaching elite knowledge. The estimated date of Memphis may be a key for a global Source Codes network.

Memphis is known as Men-nefer, Inbu-hedj, 'white walls' and Melchat-Tawy, 'brilliant lands.' Memphis played a dominant role for the Eighteenth Dynasty kings. Thutmoses V was known as 'High priest of Ptah', Amenhotep III (divinized) built the lost temple of Nebmatre, 'united with Ptah,' in the thirtieth year of his reign.

This is essential as we move into connection with Akhenaton (Amenhotep IV) and Memphis. The horizon of Aten was already used during his early years of reign. If we take for example, Mesopotamia (Babylon), it is endorsed in different major cities as Borsippi. Borsippi is described as 'another Babylon' or 'Babylon the second'. The horizon of Aten is mentioned at Memphis, Amarna and Waset (Thebes).

Let's note Akhenaton's links with Memphis. Recent excavations by Maarten

Raven's University of Leiden team, confirms with Beatrix Lohr's work during the 1970s, that the Memphite area remained a predominant religious and administrative centre during the Amarna Period. Memphis was a significant Atenist centre.

Akhenaton's focus to re-establish an older archaic cult with links to Abu Sir and Abu Ghorab deserve further investigation that may unlock missing Source Codes knowledge on the origins of ancient Egypt and the final development of power in ancient Egypt in Akhenaton and Tutankhamen.

The Pharaoh Akhenaton

'I shall make "the House of Aten" for the Aten, my father,
in Akhetaton this place.'

— AKHENATON

It is March 2012; the deal with my tour team was an arduous, seven hours bus drive to Tel-el-Armana, 250 km from the West Bank of Thebes, collecting police and army escorts on the way. At 4.30 am, I awoke wide-eyed, bounced down to breakfast to collect a roll, freshly picked west bank bananas and local honey. I knew this was going to be an epic journey once we arrived in Tel-el-Amarna to experience the next level of transformation.

I require very little sleep in Egypt and the rest of my group were not quite so enthusiastic this early on in the day. My enthusiasm and determination creates experiences at power sites, outside of the usual tourist zones, that push doors and new possibilities for each individual. The seven-hour bus journey began by winding through the biblical villages of the west bank and livestock in a backdrop of 'call to prayer'– our tour bus rattling and bouncing its way through the dusty, uneven dirt tracks with a group of sixteen, snoozing individuals.

We would then fly up the newly opened desert road at sunrise to a spectacular Sahara landscape that encompasses two thirds of Egypt. As we drew closer to Tel-el-Amarna, the nearby oasis was a spectacular, emerald green canopy of palms greeting us in ancient biblical scene of sweeping and hypnotic galabaya. Carts, donkeys and livestock were being driven patiently, nowhere, by shepherd peoples. Vast, fresh harvests of oranges, dates and bananas were piled high on battered carts. Chickens, goats and cattle – it was market day – and we were surrounded by the noise of bartering, daily business and animals.

The clock was turning back thousands of years and we were also going nowhere. Ra had, everywhere, scorched the pharaonic faces of the local peoples, etching the history of generations who had worked the land before. The bottleneck in the road *allowed us to slow right down and breathe in Egypt before we took the bustling ferry to the east bank.*

Every last moment was slowed to make a majestic entrance to Tel-el-Amarna. The ferry crossed the Nile silently as the blinding noon sun magnified the blue sky. We drove through the mud brick village of simple abodes, the children waved at us and skipped barefoot after our bus as I handed out sweets and bananas.

As we drew up the desert road to the ticket office to the entrance of Tel-el-Amarna, the dark blue police truck and its occupants came quickly to life. Akhataten, (Amarna) the immense city of Pharaoh Akhenaton and his Queen Nefertiti, is some 10 kilometres to its boundaries, hemmed in by limestone cliffs, 5 kilometres to the Nile. It is now a vast, stark expanse of foreboding desert. In the ticket office, the makeshift shops became quickly animated but Akhenaton was calling.

In Ancient Egypt, during the Eighteenth Dynasty, the Pharaoh Akhenaton reigned for only a short period, 1353-1335 BC. Originally named as Amenhotep IV, he changed his title early in his succession to Akhenaton.

This chapter is dedicated to exploring Akhenaton as a missing link and connection with The Shining Ones, and to a lost archaic knowledge. Akhenaton is a fascinating character to explore in our quest to uncover the missing links with The Shining Ones and our cosmic origins.

Akhenaton was son of Amenhotep III and his Queen, Teye. Akhenaton became king upon the death of Tutmose, so was an unlikely successor, whose grandparents were Yusa (Father of Great Royal Wife of Amenhotep III, Teye and grandmother, Truiu. Their KV46 tomb was built in the Valley of the Kings, Luxor (which is also known as Valley of the Gates of the Kings).

Akhenaton can also be possibly linked with a reburial in V5 tomb, Valley of the Kings. However, please note that this is an unproven link. Akhenaton was the last major King of this dynasty that ruled Waset (which is Ancient Thebes or Modern Luxor). During the Eighteenth Dynasty, Thebes was one of the major seats of power. The direction of Thebes was under some dominance of the Priests of Amun-Ra.

Let us recall the Amaziah peoples of Africa. These are the tribal indigenous peoples of North Africa. They regard Akh-Akh as the region of the stars; the collective abode for their ancestors is Akhu. The first King of Egypt's First Dynasty was King Akha.

We have 35,000 years BC of pre-dynastic history recorded in the Royal Papyrus of Turin. The thirteenth nome of Ancient Egypt is Annu; the later Greek for this iconic city of learning is Heliopolis – the original city that housed the original Benben stone.

The O'Briens in their book *The Genius of The Few* trace links with Akhenaton and Joseph to the Eighteenth Dynasty official, Amenhotep, son of Hapu, scribe and philosopher of Pharaoh Amenhotep III (c.1417-1379). They also make links with the spectacular Shining Ones and Moses:

> *'Akhenaton's concept of a monotheistic aten, symbolized by the sun disk was not dissimilar from the patriarchal reference of Yahweh-El Shaddai-who as Shamash, was already revered as the "sun god" in Babylon.'*

Akhenaton RC., 1353-1335, must be further acknowledged. Even Sigmund Freud, the Austrian neurologist who became the father of psychoanalysis in the Western World, traced the links with the figure of Akhenaton and Moses in his 1939 book *Moses and Monotheism.*

Akhenaton's importance is often deliberately rejected by conventional Egyptology for reasons that disclose greater truths of humanity and spirituality beyond conventionally accepted histories. It is most revealing to further investigate and explore Akhenaton's connections with The Shining Ones.

If we note the sculptures of the Amarna Period, the colossi statues were discovered in 1925 at the eastern gate of Karnak temple complex by Maurice Pillet, French architect and director of works for the Egyptian Antiquities service at Karnak.

The colossi statues of Akhenaton combine giant-size, paradoxical opposites, the alchemical male and female counterparts, the transformation of young and old. There is a profusion of opinion on Akhenaton. Who was he? How relevant is he? What did the cult of Aten represent? What does it mean today? Why was Akenhaton deliberately removed from history after his death apart from in the oracular wisdom traditions?

Akhenaton's name only resurfaced again in the mid 1820s during Napoleon's expedition of Egypt. By the mid-nineteenth century, the story was set; Akhenaton was depicted as a lunatic protagonist of monotheism contrary to incomplete evidence. This lunatic protagonist of monotheism exclusively worshipped the Aten, the solar disc.

But was Akhenaton a genius, perhaps a Shining One, dedicated to reviving and continuing archaic traditions? Was Akhenaton a living template of cosmic man?

In 1910, Arthur Weigall wrote in *The Life and Times of Akhenaton, Pharaoh of Egypt*:

> 'Akenaton's art might be said to be a kind of renaissance–a return to the classical period of archaic days; the underlying motive of this return being the desire to lay emphasis upon the king's character of that most ancient of gods, Ra Horakhti.'

In 1985, Robert Hari, Alfred Grimm, and in 2005, Herman Schlögall, suggested Osiris connections associated with The Sed Festival; once again the connection with processes of initiation and universal spiritual processes. Here, the symbolizm for individual and state is rebirth and completion. The aten symbolism is solar and lunar, masculine and feminine.

Note here the critical reference to the neutral point as gateway. This gateway has been and is continuously deliberately closed down for us. Toxic stories cannot then be filtered intelligently. Toxic stories can then be designed and manipulated. But who by? Akhenaton's father, Amenhotep III, was already divinized and symbolized as the Aten. It is also interesting to note here that Akhenaton's son, Tutankhamen (originally named as Tutankamen) is also named in his tomb as:

> 'The dynamic God, Lord of Crowns/Regalia, Nebkheprura, Son of Ra, Tutankhamun, ruler of Southern Heliopolis, living forever "like Ra everyday", the latter, as "Heka" of Horakhty Osiris, King Lord of Two Lands, Nebkheprura, justified.'

Perhaps this dynasty holds the key to bringing us closer to The Shining Ones, the concept and reality of Christ and roots of modern religions. Queen Nefertiti was the principal wife of Akhenaton. Ay was her nurse and this possibly suggests a link with Ay's family. Ancient Egyptian sources document the existence of their six children.

Meryetaten, Meketaten and Ankhsenpaaten are named, but three more daughters are undocumented. Ankhkeperure (or Smenkhkare) was the successor of Akhenaton. Tutankhamen became successor of Ankhkeperure (or Smenkhkare) and was crowned as Tutankhaton.

Tutankhamen reigned for nine years, and was nineteen years old at time of his death. There is no solid evidence in Egypt's history, and not during the Amarna period of any priestly conspiracy. This came later with religion. The corruption of the Amun priesthood of the Eighteenth Dynasty has developed from patriarchal assumptions about Egyptian religion and the priesthood since Classical times.

The notion of Egyptian priests as the initiates of secret wisdom grew rapidly in the Classical period and was revived during the Renaissance.

After the religious wars of the Reformation, a more sinister portrayal of the Egyptian priesthood arose and continues today to corrupt powerful dynastic connections. By the mid-new Kingdom the aten was well established. Tutmosis IV utilised the Aten to protect the pharaoh as a god of war.

Amenhotep III or Amenophis III encouraged the worship of the Aten, so this was not a cult uniquely shaped by Akhenaton. Late nineteenth and twentieth century scholars shaped this later.

The Aten

The words for 'MAAT' are truth and justice. It is useful to note that 'MA' is mother in all parts of the globe. This is the sound of the divine feminine! Truth and justice are the principles of Maat, who is daughter of Ra. The aten was also named 'the Prince of Maat'. Traditionally Osiris presided over final judgment: the heart was weighed against the counterbalance represented by Maat for entry to eternity.

The Aten as 'the Prince of Truth' became a source of inner guidance and personal responsibility. This takes on an exciting twist in our quest to understand the path of light, the path of the hero. Here is a groundbreaking cosmic template for man and earlier roots for later Christianity that is often hidden and deleted in conventional Egyptology.

At Akhenaton (Tel-el-Amarna), the axis of Akhenaton's tomb and a small temple of Aten both point to the sunrise of the Spring Equinox, again linking with resurrection of Osiris. The Great Pyramid also casts no shadow at midday during the Spring Equinox. This is another reference and clue to Christ, the cosmic template of man and the gateway to divinity. Akhenaton's programme for the 'Great Aten Temple' was directed in the 'House of Aten', also known as 'The Mansion of the Benben.'

The original Benben stone stood in the temple of the sun god Ra (Ra-Horakhty or 'Ra-Horus of the Horizon') at Heliopolis. Here we have deliberate connections to a much older archaic cult. Replicated Benben stones were created as obelisks and erected throughout Ancient Egypt.

The Great Benben of Ra-Horus of the horizon in the name of 'Shu who is Aten' was created by Akhenaton at Karnak Temple. At Karnak, I discovered another limestone crystal altar or 'hotep' of 'peace offerings' (similar to the crystal altar at Abu Ghorab, on the Memphis plateau). Tel-el-Amarna is 58 km (36 mi) south of the city of al-Minya, 312 km (194 mi) south of the Egyptian capital Cairo and 402 km (250 mi) north of Thebes (Luxor).

Connections with The Shining Ones can be made with Akhenaton. The Aten is a symbol of one and unity, of universe and transcendence, of both solar and lunar, of male and female, and zero point. The zero point is all important in advanced shamanic and consciousness processes that transcend time, dimensions and usual realities. Knowing Ra was equated with the aten. At Akataten (or modern Tel-el Amarna) provision was also made for The Tomb of the Mnevis Bull, that linked with Ra at Heliopolis, to be built. Maat and Shu were also incorporated into the aten.

Earlier, Aten was known as a falcon-headed anthromorphic deity, close to the earlier depictions of Ra or Ra-Horakhty. Much later, aten was depicted as a solar disc, with a uraeceus at its base and light rays with hands open or holding an ankh. Examples can be found during the reign of Amenhotep II or Amenhophis II (1427-1401 BC) as father of Akhenaton.

Akhenaton created the 'Temple of Aten' in several nomes (or areas) of Egypt; at Thebes, Akhataten, Memphis and Sesebi, Nubia. 'The room of The Seasons,' in King Niuserre's Old kingdom solar temple at Abu Ghorab, is decorated with wall paintings of the fauna and flora and the three seasons of the Egyptian year.

In the Museum of Cairo, spectacular frescos from the Palace, at Akhetaton (Tel el-Amarna) demonstrate the connection with Memphis. Nefertiti is also regarded as Hathor-Maat. Serpent power is fused with the aten in another dimension, a cosmic dimension. Time exisits in eternity 'neheh'. The metaphysical experience of light alternates with darkness, expanding and contracting with existence. Akhenaton is known as:

- *The living Horus*
- *Horus of Gold, who exacts the name of Aten*
- *Beautiful-of-Transformation-is-Re*
- *Great in his lifetime, given life forever*

Akhenaton is also importantly referenced as:

- *He is an AKH, a transfigured one, standing in the east horizon between heaven and earth.*

This takes us closer to The Shining Ones and the cosmic template of Christ.

What are Source Codes?

Ancient Egyptian knowledge, language, art, architecture and spirituality were designed as exact cosmic templates. This included man. It is fascinating to note here the spin-doctors of conventional Egyptology have generated incomplete stories based in a later patriarchal view.

The Ancient Egyptian neteru are often translated and promoted incorrectly as deities or gods. Neteru is the missing or deleted Source Codes Resource critical for consciousness and world change today and understanding the ancient world of yesterday.

The Ancient Egyptians engaged in knowledge of heaven, Earth and Duat (or Tuat). The Duat (or Tuat) is the realm of death, both physical and ritualistic which is the invisible region penetrating the living world. In the Duat exist ancestors and neteru. Entrance to this region is by inner spiritual illumination. A shamanic trilogy existed of three worlds, Celestial, Terrestrial (Malkuth) and Intermediate (Duat or Tuat).

In the Intermediate, the divine radiates as neteru. Today, we often fail to credit ancient knowledge with the magnificence it deserves. We are often restricted by incomplete stories and arrogance that we perhaps know more. Our stories often only allow a glimpse of magnificence, switching you on temporarily to what the ancients knew of the high-frequency cosmic templates and knowledge that existed beyond our time structures. Often the switch-on is momentary.

It is important to be aware that what we believe is possible in our lives is also manipulated through deliberately limiting stories of survival set in exact frequencies. This denies us entry to The Source Codes and the higher frequency cosmic templates.

The world is subtly and horrifically manipulated through low-frequency toxic stories that deny us magnificence and humanity at every level of life. I emphasize yet again that this is the story we now need to tackle if we are to enter into unprecedented magnificence of self and world change. We urgently need the next level. We urgently need the next level of transformation, the next level of awareness, the next level of manifestation, the next level of action, the next level of health and the next level of resolution.

Incomplete stories of external deities and gods deny new cosmic templates that can take us to the next level of resource for evolution and most definitely, contribution. This is the template of one and unity, essential for critical world change and healing at essential individual, and now collective levels, to accelerate new possibilities and journeys for humanity.

The ancient Egyptians were gifted entry to magnificence beyond time and the choices that cycles would bring as definitive future events. This super-simplicity is what we now need to find the right ways forward based in the themes we face and create today.

The critical inner work unlocks freedom and awareness beyond conventional paradigms, structures and time-lines. It is super-awareness that allows us to comprehend the magnificent transformation of myths and manifest it. It allows us to remember the myths that are relevant histories and truths of humanity and earth.

In low frequencies, we easily drop into unreliable awareness and repeatedly create toxic stories. Limited, we have no way of knowing what magnificence and truth is, so we accept, create and allow far less magnificence. Knowing this is critical in listening for new stories and authentic solutions in life and world whether we are thought-leaders, loving friends or parents.

Awareness can unlock magnificent stories not only for self but also for world. Our awareness has been deliberately manipulated and switched off so resolution can be arduous and challenging. Society is not wired to support your success and magnificence. Your magnificence is often not respected and honoured. Often, we absorb these toxic stories so we finally succumb to believing and manifesting less than magnificence.

I believe this is the root of all healing agendas. We often know this, but we don't know what to do to transform it. Even if you think you are aware, think again. The world is engineered in deliberately manipulated low-frequency stories to lock out your awareness, to slow evolution, to maintain survival mode, so you are locked in.

The way out is life work on high-frequency transformation and awareness processes. Awareness excellence requires high frequency and this is the vital sovereignty of empowering health, well-being, intelligence, love, manifestation and change. This is not 'soft' spirituality locked in non-relevant modern life ideas. This is a question of maintaining the magnificence that positively influences and improves your life experiences, health and resource to love and positively contribute to family, friends and community.

Changing your frequency brings the power resource to maintain magnificence, awareness and energy levels for action. Often meditation will switch on magnificence momentarily. How do we switch it on, and switch it on for good? A significant focus of my investigations is the next level of awareness and action critical for you and the world you live in every day. This is living positive change: conscious, awake, empowered.

The next level is high-frequency awareness, healing resolution and action whoever you are, whatever you do, whatever your track record. These are critical times for humanity when magnificence needs to be switched on, switched on, and switched on. Repeated cycles of trauma and conflict will not deliver the next level of magnificence. Fortunately, the ancients left us clues that are locked into these times for unlocking magnificent times now.

We can change to higher frequency, we can then change our stories, we can change the stories we hand down. You may wish to change your stories and repeat cycles but you may not have the resource for lasting success.

Let's explore how to magnify and upscale this resource.

The fully trained ancient Egyptian initiate fully understood and created *'the kingdom of heaven'*. Based on this, information becomes tantalizing when we explore what an initiate could enter and know beyond later religious constraints. I propose that this takes us into the beginning, before toxic stories, unlocking the awareness and high frequency that reveals this. But what is an initiate? According to *The New Oxford Dictionary, www.oed.com* in 2014, *an initiate* is defined as:

- *To begin, commence, and enter upon; to introduce, get going, give rise to, originate, 'start' (a course of action, practice, etc.). b. intr. To take its beginning, commence.*
- *To admit (a person) with proper introductory rites or forms into some society or office, or to knowledge of or participation in some principles or observances, esp. of a secret or occult character; hence more generally, to introduce into acquaintance with something, to instruct in the elements of any subject or practice.*
- *To perform the first rite; to take the initiative. b. To undergo or receive 'initiation'.*

Life *can* present a story of magnificent initiation, resolution and opportunities during critical times. Based on this, the following information becomes tantalizing. When we enter magnificence, we succeed in magnificence and we create in magnificence whatever we experience. When we enter The Source Codes we finally crack low-frequency stories.

- High frequencies create timely miracles even in the most challenging of life experiences. Hit the high-frequency button again and again!
- Frequency can create gradual transformation, awareness and evolution. Higher frequency will accelerate natural healing processes, bending

time and improving results of transformation, awakening and manifestation. Hit the high-frequency button for effective results!

- Frequency can also deliberately hijack evolution if we allow it. Be aware if you hit low frequencies, create the space and time to process and hit the high-frequency button. Only you can choose change by surrendering to and mastering it. Your history is the critical foundation of change. You will power and accelerate through challenging life experiences with greater ease. Priceless!

These are very real and very significant facts that affect magnificence of life, health and world change. This is the essential foundation of high-frequency living and re-writing our stories and future in *THE SOURCE CODES*.

CHAPTER 4

The Science on Meditation and High-frequency Magnificence

Fast forward into the twenty-first century, and meditation is a vast arena bringing varied technologies and success for increasing intelligence, health and potential. In order to upscale the value of meditation we are going to consider the scientific evidence and benefits.

Scientific studies deliver the proof for benefits but what you also need to know is meditation can range from simple relaxation techniques over a vast spectrum, to outstanding inner change, well-being and health excellence. Which approach, is often a vital question and agenda for many individuals seeking answers and solutions. Meditation can re-design your transformation, awakening and human potential. Meditation can accelerate your transformation and awareness processes if you engage correctly with the technologies.

Groundbreaking inner change in meditation can out-perform conventional time structures, defy or shift existing scientific explanation. Without regular awareness practice limited results can persist. Meditation can ignite outstanding pro-evolution perspectives and solutions.

Two lines of investigation will be explored in this book. First, exploring stories of ancient knowledge and lost technologies that out-manoeuvre time, evolving and bypassing conventional paradigms for self and world solutions. Second, the question of generating and maintaining incredible inner-change of greater healing and awareness processes, core-emotional strengthening and potentials of mission and health.

Meditation practitioners and ardent fans, what if a bigger project is introduced beyond time consuming self-agenda coping strategies for stress and rebalance in modern life? Certainly, it's an essential industry. Drukman and Swets (1988) estimated $300 billion a year was spent on training and development courses on human potential in the USA alone. It is some way towards creating a better individual.

Coping strategies do reach desired freedom momentarily then energy levels drop back into stress stories. What if technologies could be upgraded to deliver beyond endless loops of coping strategies? What if you knew 'how to' be free? What if the big project is more magnificence in life and the world? This would be ground-breaking! Self and world is often not designed to deliver freedom to such a level of magnificence and success! What about a re-design?

According to Abraham Maslow's *Hierarchy of Needs* only 2% of the population is free. This story often filters into life and human potential technologies even today. If this is correct, this signifies problems because who are the 2% who are free? Maslow's Hierarchy of Needs states that we must satisfy each need in turn, starting with the first, which deals with the most obvious needs for survival itself.

First stage is level one: biological and physiological needs; air, food, drink, shelter, warmth, sex, sleep, second is level two: safety needs – protection from environment, security, order, law, limits, stability; third is level three: belonging and love - work group, family, affection, relationships; fourth is level four: esteem needs – self-esteem, achievement, mastery, independence, status, dominance, prestige, managerial responsibility; and fifth, level five: self-actualization – personal potential, self-fulfilment, seeking personal growth and peak experiences.

Who is making the decisions about your stories? Even in the human potential field old structures exist, often directed by inexperienced facilitators who have 'opted in' to gathering second-hand expert knowledge but 'opted out' of awareness and practice that ultimately delivers essential freedom of an individual and a non-generic approach. The individual approach is super-effective. The diluted generic approach can be a minefield of time-consuming limited successes.

This is why searching, longing and dreaming is also part of the story. Human potential facilitators often restrict because of inability to see your bigger picture story (perhaps still in the 98%). There is an alternative paradigm of success and freedom that includes all your stories. If the major design flaw of humanity is in the focus of repeated stories and cycles in pain, suffering and failing (that's a whopping 98% majority) then there is so much that can be improved.

Remodeling this design fault at every level can tackle immense individual and global conflict. Here is an interesting fact. Back in 2001, the Director of The World Health Organisation, Gro Harlem, predicted that depression, ranked then at number four in 2001 would jump to number 2 by 2020 as one of the leading causes of global burden of disease due to rising number of violent conflicts, war, displacements, disasters, political instability, violence against women and children and HIV. Four hundred and fifty million people were affected in 2001.

Then the World Health Organisation was playing a critical role in global mental health action; essential in human development and poverty reduction. In 2001, 40% of countries had no mental health policy in place, 30% of countries had no mental health programme and 90% of countries did not include children. These are mind-blowing statistics.

Solutions and effective technologies for health and well-being that relates to vision and progress must be developed. In 2014, the cost of stress was $300 billion dollars to the USA alone. In the USA, 70 million people have high blood pressure that costs $130 billion a year to treat. 75% of health care spending in the USA is on preventable chronic illness. Heart disease, stroke, cancer, respiratory diseases and diabetes accounted for 36 million global deaths in 2008. 80% can be prevented!

Depression affected more than 350 million individuals globally in 2014. The statistics are incredible; affecting lives, health and progression. Depression affects generation after generation in limiting stories: limiting potential and potential change. This is absolutely pivotal for good and positive world change. It is a crucial time to create contribution and solutions for this bigger challenge and crisis of humanity.

⌁

Dubbed 'The Medicine Buddha' by Tibetan Buddhists, Nobel Prize winning biochemist, Elizabeth Blackburn created an unusual and yet groundbreaking research partnership with Elizabeth Epel, a postdoc from UCSF's Psychiatry Department, with an interest in the damage done by chronic stress.

In the 1980s, Blackburn discovered an enzyme called telomerase that protects and builds telomeres – this is key in the process of ageing and anti-ageing. In 2014, Epel, is Director of The Ageing, Metabolism and Emotion Centre citing her influence by maverick holistic-health thinker Dr Deepak Chopra.

With blood samples of 58 women, 2 groups of stressed mothers and controls, the research results were startling. The greater the stress, the shorter their telomeres and lower the levels of telomerase. Their research led to trials researching the link between meditation and telomerase. This is fascinating research that may motivate you further. Short telomeres results linked age-related conditions and disease such as osteoarthritis, diabetes, obesity, heart disease, Alzheimer's and strokes.

Blackburn is convinced stress matters. She and Epel, have demonstrated the effects of stress during pregnancy on telomeres that can be passed on to the next generation. Here, stressed mothers' birth children having shorter telomeres. This is super-fascinating as there is a direct contradiction with existing paradigms that traits are passed via genes. This is vital information in gathering more knowledge on how stories are passed. This is an exciting story in the world of holistic health. This is super-exciting in a world where meditation is change for good.

Just think about the future health and human potential benefits of unborn children. Once again we journey in another story that releases decades of limited stories, igniting new possibilities and alternative scenarios of hardship and economic costs.

Simple pro-health meditation programmes could be implemented for improving future generations. These super-stress-busting technologies really work!

On *www.bloomberg.com*, Katherine Burton and Anthony Effinger write, '*To make a killing on Wall Street, start meditating*', May 2014.

This article brings a fashionable, contemporary twist to the ancient art of meditation when many of us are struggling to make the bills each month. Even Wall Street is looking for new strategies to create new paradigms. The Little Buddha of Wall Street, David Ford, hedge-fund manager works with 20 minutes of meditation each day. In two years he has made more money than ever before. His event driven credit fund, Lahgo Partners LP, increased by 24% in 2013. So what is in meditation for us? We will be taking journeys with meditation, in Book Two, on successfully improving our lives.

Dalio, 64, runs the largest hedge-fund firm in the world and is worth $14 billion dollars according to Bloomberg's Billionaires Index. He pays half the cost of meditation programmes for the employees at his Connecticut-based, Bridgewater Associates LP. Now this is really contributing to positive world change. He has agreed to give most of his fortune to charity under the Giving Pledge Programme started by Bill Gates and Warren Buffet.

The cool contemporary twist is not a new one. During the nineteenth century's, Industrial Revolution, philanthropy and meditation practices went hand in hand in The British Empire. Global Corporate, Google, offers 'Search Inside Yourself', a programme created by Chade-Meng tan, a Google employee and author of 'Search Inside Yourself; the unexpected path to Achieving Success, Happiness and World Peace'.

Meditation is no longer a post-hippie new age soft topic rapidly fashionable once again in the mainstream. The focus is on increased profits, better decision-making, health and stress reduction, leadership and workplace affectivity. Nike and Proctor and Gamble have mindfulness programmes in place. But remember this is not a new idea. Einstein was a Theosophist, Queen Victoria a spiritualist and Da Vinci, an alchemist.

Queen Victoria led the way when her beloved King died. The elite and eminent followed her lead in spiritualism and even the Society of Physical Research was supported by Government and science. Gladstone declared spiritualism as the leading science of the day.

Let's look at more science behind the reasons why we should meditate. Sara Lazar, Ph.D., MGH Psychiatric Neuroimaging, Harvard University has demonstrated in 2011, in research via only an eight weeks programme of meditation, that meditation rapidly changes the way neurons communicate and changes brain structure. Her scientific research further validates meditation technologies.

Here is what she discovered. Meditation slows age decline (increasing the cortex size of a 50-year -old to that of a 25-year-old after only eight weeks of meditation). Meditation affects the hippocampus, increasing learning, memory and executive decision-making. Meditation activates the tempero pridal junction increasing perspective, empathy and compassion. Meditation decreases the size of the migduala and regulates stress and perspective to environmental stress factors.

Let us revisit this list of pro-meditation benefits. With dedicated and regular practice these are the possible benefits of meditation:

- Transforming sadness, anger and depression.
- Transforming loss of interest, passion, vision of self and world view.
- Transforming guilt and low self-esteem.
- Transforming tiredness and motivational issues.
- Increasing the value and health of every individual globally.
- Increasing memory, learning, time management, creative solutions, awareness.
- Anti-ageing.
- Transforming stress-related health issues such as diabetes, blood pressure, obesity, skin conditions, poor digestion, appetite and poor energy levels.
- Transforming stress-related society issues, loving family and community relationships, workplace productivity and relationships, female and male power stereotypes.
- Happiness and well-being, positive self vision, positive world contribution, collaboration, connectedness and inner peace.
- Upgrading your mission in greater positive and good.
- Transforming outdated structures of thinking and unresolved trauma.
- Can ignite the energy for positive change, maintaining positive change.

In this book the definition of meditation is positive, bringing renewed self-awareness and world-awareness processes, technologies and daily activities. In

Book Two, the meditations can be practiced by absolutely anyone at any level and applied to any life area for improving intelligence, inner peace and transformation, potential, motivation and responsible action.

The practitioner should be mindful of positive self and world focus, in dedicated practice and in life. Meditation is a human potential excellence technology for all, regardless of age, origin, status and wealth. The foundation of any meditation practice starts with self. Meditation is a journey of awareness of deep self-understanding, regulated by truth, intelligence, responsibility and love.

Understanding alchemy plays a vital role in this research, Candice Pert, Ph.D., with Nancy Marriot in *The Science of Emotions and Consciousness*, 2007, explores how consciousness and unconscious mind penetrate and influence every aspect of the physical body and life.

According to Pert, emotions are material and immaterial, are physical and can be weighed. Emotions vibrate with an electrical charge, physical and psychological, coordinating the entire body-mind.

Can intentional transformational and meditation processes result in, not only unlocking consciousness but also unlocking and accelerating conventional consciousness structures and time frameworks? Can advanced alchemical processes permit new awareness; in turn, unlock new possibilities and cohesion with new realities or new dimensions? Often, advanced meditation techniques transform ground-breaking inner vision.

But what happens when new upgraded super-consciousness and new super-energy levels are unlocked. Does this create ground-breaking cohesion that affects how we experience new realities beyond usual structures? Perhaps a massive electrical charge of emotions can be photographed and filmed as orbs phenomena during advanced meditation and transformation. This is certainly one possibility.

Interestingly, Dr Erik Richard Kandel (b.1929) was awarded a Nobel Prize in Physiology or Medicine in 2000, when he proved that memory resides at the level of the receptor. Memory storage is in your spinal cord as well as throughout your body-mind. Memories are conscious and unconscious-mediated by the molecules of emotion (high-energy/low-energy charge).

Meditation and transformation excellence can affect buried unconscious memories unlocking high charge positive emotions. Memories buried far below awareness will affect perception, decisions, behaviour and health in low-energy charge emotions. Energy healers often call this emotional trauma. It is this core emotional trauma that limits and slows vitality, awareness, perception, decisions, behaviour and relationships, intelligence, happiness and health.

Emotional trauma must be successfully transformed before any Psi potential excellence. (This is an important note for Psi research.) Research has found that regular, intensive, advanced meditation and transformation that targets core emotional trauma and high-frequency change for super-consciousness, whilst remaining body awake, is most effective. This increases awareness, cohesion, inner peace, accelerated transformation processes, responsibility, emotional intelligence, positive contribution, positive health and well-being benefits.

This is an alchemy process of accelerated transformation and awareness pathways. This is the path of the initiate, mystic, shaman or visionary.

The PAG (Periaqueductal gray) is a structure in the brain that sets pain thresholds. Neurons in the frontal cortex project into the PAG, and this makes conscious control possible over pain and alertness. This indicates how one can choose how to interpret stimulus. For example, positive thoughts affect and create positive healing. *You can create a positive journey of transformation.*

You can become involved in a positive narrative to promote health and well-being that potentially heals one's physiology. The body-mind is a vast network of communicating molecules.

This creates a positive healing cycle, increasing health and awareness of choice and responsibility. Here is another key, in understanding how to unlock groundbreaking accelerated transformation. We have much more control not only over health but, awareness and the world around us. We can choose to activate positive high-frequency emotions, improving health and potential, then world change possibilities (self-transformation processes come first). A very different solution but a tangible one, and one ancient wisdom has described for millennia.

This is tantalizing and explains why similar frequency stories and cycles are played out time and time again. Why do certain individuals have extra-sensory abilities and others simply do not? Emotional energy charge improves abilities; alchemists, mystics and shamans have known this for millennia. What happens when we change frequency to change the story?

As human beings we experience high-frequency super-consciousness states of bliss and infinite love as gateways to magnificence. This is built into our anatomy and, however rare these experiences, we all fall in love. Science proves we have a capacity to create a positive vision for humanity and planet if we choose.

There are many states of consciousness: awake, sleeping, dreaming, meditative, emotional states and alert. Consciousness is every aspect of how you experience and understand reality. It can encompass infinite, new frontiers (if this is your vision) or finite potential (if this is your vision). It can hold the key to incredible human potential and new world frontiers.

When we awaken and evolve positive belief structures we hold the resource to live vibrantly and consciously. You hold the key to inner freedom whatever your life situation. Perhaps this is simply concluded by Dawson Church Ph.D., author of *The Genie in your Genes: Epigenetic Medicine* and *The New Biological Intention*, in his essay "Psychological Clearing as Prelude to Soul Emergence":

> *'When your ears aren't filled with the chatter of reactivity and cacophony of negativity, and your life is free of stress generated mindless actions and the prolonged cleanup operations that result from the subsequent mess, then the still small voice of spirit may be heard. Imagine if all the world were healed. Imagine if all emotional traumas were tapped away, and everyone's physical health blossomed. Imagine if we no longer had to deal with all the challenges that rush at us as the result of the unhealed emotional wounds of others, and we were free to play our own creative, harmonic music.*
>
> *Imagine if war and poverty vanished, as social traumas (which are nothing more than individual traumas writ large) disappear, as the urge to strike and hurt others dissipates in the experience of divine love. Twenty years ago, I could not imagine such a world. Today, I expect us humans as a species to achieve it within my lifetime.'*

Almost all cultures worldwide have a form or practice to develop awareness of the moment in prayer, ceremony, ritual, mantra, yoga, tai chi, chi gong, martial arts and meditation. Intentional awareness transforms lives and alleviates suffering, improves capacity to control or regulate emotions, transform emotional dysfunction, evolve and refine emotional programming, decreases negative vision and perspective, reduce depression, changing the imbalance of circuits in the brain.

Here are the positive benefits: healing, immune response, stress-reduction, physical health, happiness and well-being. Self-awareness becomes refined awareness and individuals enter improved world vision. This creates a journey of self-care, self-love and world awareness that increasingly develops. This shifts the lens of focus from self-limiting stories of self and world perception.

However, my investigations reveal that only *regular* practice creates outstanding results.

This brings questions on which meditation and transformation technologies to use to impact significant benefits. Super-meditation technologies accelerate super-transformation for exclusive entry into new possibilities. Regularly applied super-meditation unlocks super-awareness and mastery for magnificence and extra-sensory potential that we often describe as miracles.

Advanced meditation and transformation technologies affect change beyond slower structures, pain cycles and transform profound inner vision. This is key to incredible inner and outer world change. Super-energy is multi-dimensional and wires in the Source Codes to ignite unity. Low frequency denies access to The Source Codes and ultimately unity.

The Source Codes is where super-consciousness potential is. Incredible awareness and human potential that actions powerful self and world change, resides here. This has been core to my research and training programmes. This takes us into the science of super-consciousness technologies to create groundbreaking possibilities in healing, awareness and even training methods that create proven excellence and essential human potential breakthroughs.

This could lead to some interesting directions in brain wave analysis of potential research candidates for improved scientific testing. Happiness and well-being, empowerment and confidence, human potential and excellence are instrumental keys in new extra-sensory abilities that can increase phenomenon.

This is important in increasing scientific evidence and making connections between orbs phenomena, super-consciousness states and human potential excellence. This can be described as 'unlocking', 'reconfiguring' or 're-wiring' to achieve important cohesion with The Source Codes.

This is the power of one and unity. In awakening an individual into the internal lens of focus, this impacts how powerfully an individual can influence reality, in the same way yogis, shamans and mystics do. It indicates that cohesion is absolutely necessary for increasing extra-sensory abilities and phenomena. This has profound implications for thought leaders and influencers of positive, conscious change.

We need to transcend the conventional Western view that meditation is only for relaxation; often meditation benefits are understood as only coping strategies for stress, blood pressure and depression. However, scientific evidence suggests meditation can physically change brain functioning to preserve and enhance learning and cognitive functions. Here the impact is biological with positive implications for neurodegenerative disease improving motor control and cognition.

The Dalai Lama, aware of neuroplasticity's potential, offered eight of Tibetan Buddhism's most experienced and advanced monks of meditation training to be EEG scientifically tested against a group of non-meditators by Davidson et al (2004).

The Tibetan Buddhist monks had between 10,000 and 50,000 hours of advanced meditation training. Davidson was interested in measuring Gamma waves, highest frequency or high charge energy. It is well known that the brain can generate 10 watts of electrical power. Gamma waves are greater than 40 Hertz. Delta waves are low frequency, below 4 Hertz. Alpha waves are 8-13 Hertz. Beta waves are 15-40 Hertz.

Gamma waves create highest frequency, high energy charge and create higher mental activity, perception, awareness and consciousness. Gamma waves are essential in effective nerve cell communication.

High amplitude Gamma waves and synchronizations are produced and achieved during advanced meditation training and practice by advanced practitioners. Meditation serves as a form of mental exercise that restructures the brain, redistributing gray matter. Here, the nerve centres are located.

Davidson discovered that the advanced Tibetan Buddhist monks showed greater activation of Gamma waves activity involving potentially thousands of nerve cells moving at extremely high speeds in cohesion. This movement was more coordinated than in the non-meditating novice group. The non-meditating novices showed only slight increase of Gamma activity compared with the Tibetan Buddhist monks group. Davidson discovered that brain size would be larger due to more nerve cells firing in synchronisation, and thought to play a crucial role in memory, learning and relationships.

Buddhists believe that a well-trained mind will bring peace to both individual and world. As this Buddhist concept is discussed, it brings to focus a fifty-eight people meditation for world peace and healing. This was the finale focus of Celestial Healing, in Tokyo, January 2014. I was teaching on conscious meditation connecting multiple earth power sites. The focus was on World Peace, The Great Pyramid complex, Giza, Egypt and Mt Fuji, Japan.

During the final five minutes, the four neteru: Osiris, Isis, Hathor and Horus were engaged. We focused upon Japan's major Shinto Goddess, Amateresu-ōmikami. When we opened our eyes, post-meditation synchronicity occurred which moved participants to tears. Mount Fuji emerged from weeks of winter clouds in minutes, in perfect view from the seminar room, and the sunset lighting the sky behind this magnificent earth power site.

Mount Fuji is an important earth power and gateway for healing East and West. In synchronicity, transformation spontaneously occurred in that moment. The miraculous moment was understood as a great sign of Amateresu-ōmikami.

Whether one believes in this synchronicity or not, an incredible focus for world peace and healing was created for those present and awake in that moment. The seminar perfectly ended at five o'clock as a shared moment of transformational synchronicity. Tears unlocked further transformation.

CHAPTER 5

The Science That Manifests You
as A Catalyst of Change

During email communication with Klaus Heinemann, co-author of *The Orb Project* (with Miceal Ledwith), the question of how I had filmed groundbreaking film footage was discussed. Heinemann had collected thousands and thousands of images but nothing at this level. The live film phenomenon defied conventional explanations. It was way outside of the box even in my field.

We are often all too easily swayed by knowledge assuming we know, and yet seldom fly in awesome transformation and spirituality experiences that literally turn life and world around forever. It was this I wanted to share. This is exactly what I had been looking for. I knew this is exactly what every individual was also looking for behind the safety net of basking in someone else's knowledge. And that is exactly it! I wasn't thinking of random peak experiences that make us hunger for more.

If we understand how, then we can use The Source Codes for super-accelerating human potential, the critical source of reliable solutions for future generations. We would also be right on track for groundbreaking positive change that would tackle generations of inaction and ineffective knowledge that repeats the same destructive and limiting stories. *If only people were more conscious of how thought shapes reality and impacts humanity!*

I have always been fascinated in how awareness and transformation technologies can work more effectively and this put me ahead of the game. I wasn't a scientist interested in how The Source Codes worked but a trained 'child to adult' meta-physician who knew how The Source Codes worked. I was hooked to unravel this mystery further and share the power of The Source Codes.

The more I shared, the bigger The Source Codes resource. I became passionate about responsibility for switching on The Source Codes; who we are in the world we live and create in, and the impact we have in the short time we spend on this planet. I began recognizing frequency is the massive missing part no matter what we think we know...and no one can fake this.

This is the VIP entry to our sovereignty and freedom no matter what! The race to acquire knowledge must be met with a sovereignty of consciousness that is also 100% pro-humanity. The missing work is internal –recognizing and changing our stories! These are the stories of incomplete and corrupt histories still being created today. Only then, entry to The Source Codes is granted! Not once or a seldom entry, this is not the purpose of Celestial Healing, but repeatedly, to shift frequency into the visible and positive self and world change that is so critical now!

On 21 March 2011, Spring Equinox, 16 minutes of live, energy orbs and inter-dimensional communication was filmed at the Mortuary Temple of Rameses III, Egypt.

Researching existing and new frontiers of human potential and world change has led investigations into the questions of 'why' and 'how'. How is excellence in meditation and transformational processes achieved, beyond simple relaxation, mediocre coping strategies and slower healing processes? 'Why', and 'how', meditation and transformation technologies can and should be improved to unlock magnificent new frontiers of self and world.

How is awareness increased beyond outdated conventional limited thinking? How is awareness increased to upscale the potential of meditation and healing technologies? 'Why' and 'how' to shift repeat pain-focus to increase magnificence and excellence. When this is achieved, new frontiers are opened. Trained or gifted individuals can achieve concise scientific results in remote viewing, telepathy, transformation, ESP and intentional manifestation and phenomena, repeatedly.

How is repeated evidence of orbs phenomena and super-consciousness increased? How can super-consciousness frontiers be further accelerated? How is human potential excellence accelerated and maintained? How do advanced meditation and transformation processes influence non-conventional phenomena, time structures and even gravitational force?

This becomes incredibly important in super-consciousness research and how we achieve better transformation results and scientific evidence.

Since 1999, my role as international teacher, healer and visionary is investigating the development of high-frequency training technologies for super-consciousness potential. Blavatsky 1831–1891 (Theosophical Society), Bailey 1880-1949 (Lucis Trust) and Cayce 1877–1945 (ARE) are historically relevant healing, psychic and humanity visionaries within the early history of consciousness, human potential and contribution.

Each have in common; excellence in super-consciousness training and mastery that produced volumes of works. Each one is regarded as demonstrating exceptional and powerful, Psi, channeling and healing abilities and organisations that still influence today. These individuals are timeless visionaries for new worlds, new humanity ideas and ideals. What they also have in common is a vision of super-consciousness mastery for service to humanity. All are thought-leaders and ancient wisdom researchers with the gift of exceptional visionaries and healers.

Between 1999–2014, I completed fourteen thousand individual Life Vision Consultations and trained thirty thousand individuals. My research points to the benefits of training excellence to achieve human potential excellence for positive world contribution.

My investigations expose 'how to' unlock self from outdated low-frequency belief structures that can freeze evolution, potential and contribution. The Individual is then freed within outdated structures. This unlocks high frequency for living and health excellence. Meditation and transformation training programmes were created to increase groundbreaking self-change, igniting resource to change the critical frequency of stories.

Aware of clients' repeated unsuccessful transformation processes, I noted transformation processes can be improved with better trained facilitators and transformation-committed individuals. *Consciousness becomes the excellence key.* It is not only life stories but also resolution frequency that needs to be understood for effective healing. Individual potential increases, then the second phase of transformation unlocks world awareness and effective contribution.

I set about pioneering training structures for super-transformation and then, super-consciousness abilities, then intentional phenomena possibilities. I applied repeated positive change focus to accelerate critical processes of self-transformation. The transformation process was completed and repeated in multiples within one cycle of transformation to achieve better results. I applied super-transformation and meditation processes for resolution excellence.

The results indicate greater transformation beyond pain-cycle focus, limiting beliefs and thinking (often in repeated unresolved cycles). Conventional beliefs, thinking and time structures are locked into specific frequencies that are absorbed, and can limit or unlock new frontiers of self. I discovered increased transformation results are achieved with regular, advanced practice within training programmes and regular inner work maintenance. Frequency locks or unlocks critical potential and awareness.

My investigation questions: what can an individual achieve beyond conventional focus of meditation and transformation technologies? For example, conventional approaches include modern life coping strategies, repeated low-frequency pain-focus, stress-focus, slow ineffective transformation, basic relaxation techniques only, survival only strategies, high sensitivity, questionable energy excellence, repeated emotional and health related issues, awareness of life stories yet ineffective transformation results.

~

I said earlier that Nobel Prize winning biochemist, Elizabeth Blackburn created an unusual and yet groundbreaking research partnership with Elizabeth Epel, a postdoc from UCSF's Psychiatry Department, with an interest in the damage done by chronic stress.

With blood samples of 58 women, two groups of stressed mothers and controls, the research results were startling. The greater the stress, the shorter their telomeres and lower the levels of telomerase. Their research led to trials researching the link between meditation and telomerase. This is fascinating research that may motivate, shorter telomeres results linked age-related conditions such as osteoarthritis, diabetes, obesity, heart disease, Alzheimer's and strokes.

This is vital information in gathering more knowledge on how stories are passed. This is an exciting story in the world of holistic health. This is super-exciting in a world where meditation is change for good. Just think about the future health and human potential benefits of unborn children.

Once again we journey in another story that release decades of limited stories, igniting new possibilities and alternative scenarios of hardship and economic costs. Simple pro-health meditation programmes could be implemented for improving future generations.

The stress-busting technologies can really work! Here is the scientific evidence that stories and cycles are inherited. The next phase of the research takes us into super-consciousness investigations.

What results when an individual uses meditation and transformation excellence for inner work and Psi research? Can an individual intentionally influence orbs phenomena? What occurs when a group of advanced meditators work together? In *China's Super Psychics*, Paul Dong described an amazing example of Extra High Functioning (EHF), that happened on 1st April 1994 in the Beijing Signal Corps auditorium: Within only 30 minutes, Colonol Fu Songshan succeeded in opening more than a thousand flower buds that people held in their hands, thus speeding up time.

Between 1936 and 1955, Tsien Hsueshen received his Ph.D. at Caltech under the supervision of Dr. von Karmen, and developed the Jet Propulsion Laboratory (JPL), participated in the Manhattan Project, and earned special recognition as one of the top rocket scientists in the US. Despite his genius, Dr. Tsien was deported to China against his will during McCarthyism.

Upon his arrival in China, Tsien became one of the greatest minds behind China's technological and scientific advances in the 20th century. He developed programmess and advance university science training throughout China. Dr. Tsien attended demonstrations by groups of special Chinese citizens, 'super psychics' who could demonstrate exceptional mind-over-matter abilities. Tsien established labs within many of China's universities, to study and analyse these abilities. Dr. Tsien said:

> 'If this [phenomenon] is true, everything we know about science is wrong.'

Ms. Chulin Sun, has worked in agricultural laboratories. She utilizes her EHF abilities (Extra High Functioning / Enhanced Human Faculties - super-awareness, super-healing, super-manifestation) to accelerate the germination of seeds for developing robust seed stock for China's marginal agricultural growing areas. Ms. Sun enters a trance state in which it is observed that she moves into a different time and space. She accelerates the time for sprouting dry seeds from three to four days, to 10 minutes, generating a sprout growth of 3 to 4 inches.

> 'When David Steindl-Rast, a Benedictine monk, proposed investigating the "rainbow body", a phenomenon in which the corpses of highly developed spiritual individuals reputedly vanish, within days of death, he received an enthusiastic response from Marilyn Schlitz, IONS's director of research... "If we can establish as an anthropological fact," says Steindl-Rast, "that what is described in the resurrection of Jesus has not only happened to others, but is happening today, it would put our view of human potential in a completely different light..." Steindl-Rast's own curiosity about the rainbow body began when he heard various stories of Tibetan masters who had, through their practices, reached a high degree of wisdom and compassion. It was reported to him that when they died, rainbows suddenly appeared in the sky. "And I was told that after several days their bodies disappeared."
>
> — *IONS REVIEW, No. 59, March-May 2002*

An individual can improve Psi results because of transformation and meditation excellence. What happens when an advanced meditator enters groundbreaking high-frequency super-consciousness to throw off low-frequency reality restrictions? Can an individual influence reality? The answer is yes. Yogi Master, B.K.S. Ivyengar (14 December 1918 – 20 August 2014) describes the kundalini as the divine cosmic force, symbolized as a coiled serpent dormant in the last nerve centre at the base of the spinal column – the Shushumna.

When kundalini rises up through the chakras to the Sahasrara, the thousand-petalled lotus in the head, the yogi is in union with the Supreme Universal Soul – entering The Source Codes. This is a high-frequency Kundalini process that ignites foundations of transformation and spirituality change. And excellence. Source Codes activation allows you to master inner reality and enter the world of Yogi and Mystic to master time and reality. For you, as positive change-maker.

Kundalini is a natural process of tangible life force awakened through each energy centre or chakra. Each is a gateway that activates powerful psychological and physical transformation that increases health and well-being. A range of experiences will occur at these levels should the kundalini process be authentically activated.

It is a process of intensive transformational processes that rebalances low-frequency trauma encrypted in the physical body and energy field through each energy centre. Kundalini may be described as chi, ki, prana, life-force, serpent energy, divine force, light, consciousness or spirit.

It can be activated spontaneously or with yoga, meditation, psychedelic drugs, plant medicine, subtle energy healing, spiritual awakening, detox programmes, 'out of body experiences' and 'near death experiences', and pineal neuropsychology research. Today, regular meditation practice can increase health excellence.

'Daily rhythms in physiological and behavioural processes are controlled by a network of circadian clocks. In mammals, at the top of the network is a master clock located in the suprachiasmatic nuclei (SCN) of the hypothalamus. The SCN clock tightly controls the nocturnal synthesis and release of melatonin by the pineal gland. Several roles of melatonin in the circadian system have been identified. As a major hormonal output, melatonin distributes temporal cues generated by the SCN to the multitude of tissues expressing melatonin receptors. In some target tissues,

these melatonin signals can drive daily rhythmicity that would otherwise be lacking.'

— *P. PÉVET, The internal time-giver role of melatonin. A key for our health.*

The pineal gland is activated during kundalini experiences. It is worth noting here that intensive meditation practice will activate and maintain a healthier pineal gland and impact and progress spirituality, well-being and health excellence.

The pineal gland is known as the pineal body, conarium or epiphysis cerebri, and is a small endocrine gland in our brain. The pineal produces melatonin, a serotonin-derived hormone that affects the modulation of sleep patterns in both seasonal and circadian rhythms. The shape resembles a tiny pine cone that is also a universal symbol of antiquity. It is located in the epithalamus near the centre of the brain, between the two hemispheres.

Renes Descartes (31 March 1596 – 11 February 1650) describes the pineal gland as 'the seat of the soul' central to his pineal neurophysiology and pineal neuropsychology investigations and ideas. Today regular meditation practice can increase health excellence but the function of the pineal gland is also affected by high levels of calcification found in multiple lifestyle choices that we may not be aware of.

This calcification can have a profound affect upon spirituality progress, well-being and health excellence. Let's take a look at what calcification is and the effects of it. In the 1990s, a British scientist, Jennifer Luke, discovered that fluoride accumulates to high levels in the pineal gland. As a result of the ageing process and exposure to toxins, the pineal gland begins to calcify. This does not aid us when we are starting a journey of meditation practice and wish to continue this process in maximum health benefits.

Sodium fluoride is the primary enemy of a healthy pineal gland. This toxin is in water supplies, non-organic food and toothpaste. Mercury levels in vaccinations and dental amalgam, processed foods; caffeine, tobacco, alcohol and refined sugars can also cause and increase calcification. Technology, cell phones and wi-fi networks, can also increase and accelerate this damage.

Yet there is also super-positive news; meditation can increase melatonin levels; impacting health and well-being excellence. As synchronizer of the biological clock, melatonin is a powerful free-radical scavenger and antioxidant discovered in 1993. Melatonin is an antioxidant that can easily cross cell membranes and the blood–brain barrier. Melatonin works with other antioxidants to improve the overall effectiveness of each antioxidant. Melatonin has been proven to be twice as active as vitamin E, believed to be the most effective lipophilic antioxidant. Studies suggest that melatonin might be useful fighting infectious disease including HIV, bacterial infections, and the treatment of cancer. The Centro de Investigación Biomédica de Occidente del Instituto Mexicano del Seguro Social, Guadalajara, Jalisco, México discovered that because melatonin is multifunctioning, it could theoretically intervene at any of a number of sites in the brain to abate the changes associated with the development of Alzheimer's Disease. N-dimethyltryptamine (DMT) is produced by the pineal gland.

Dr. Rick Strassman, author of *DMT, The Spirit Molecule*, suggests the pineal gland produces DMT during mystical experiences and birth and death processes. DMT production is associated with shamanic plant medicine, lucid dreaming, peak experiences, creativity and imagination that can takes us to the critical next level.

In *Lost Secrets of the Sacred Ark*, Lawrence Gardiner states that the Pineal Eye or Third Eye is a metamorphic eye. In Yogic teaching and practice, this eye is significant in awakening awareness. He explains further that in Hinduism, it is believed that everyone has a Third Eye, a channel for sacred powers, located behind the forehead. This channel is the ultimate source of achieving enlightenment.

In Hermetic law of the Ancient Egyptian Mystery Schools, akhu or spiritual enlightenment is achieved by the raising of the kundalini through thirty- three vertebra of the spine to activate the pineal gland.

The first explorers, Caliph Al-Ma'mum of the ninth century, discovered in the King's Chamber, the same lidless sarcophagus and less widely reported, grains of aluminium silicate.

> *'The Plant of Birth was a purely symbolic tree (like the Tree of Life) from which, in accordance with the Sumerian King List (c.2000 BC), the kings were said to have been fed. Its representation was directly concerned with the Mesopotamian Gra-al: the nectar of excellence called the Gold of the Gods, which was a designation of the goddess Hathor in Egypt.'*

According to *www.crucible.org*, Colloidal Gold is linked with the following benefits. It is fascinating to note what these benefits could be if health excellence was already established:

- *General feeling of well-being and raised energy levels*
- *Enhancement of the body's natural defences against illness*

- *Increased vitality and longevity*
- *Improved glandular function*
- *Physical relaxation*
- *Repair of damaged DNA*
- *Reduced joint inflammation*
- *Relief of pain*
- *Anti-inflammatory effects*
- *Anti-depressant effects*

Some of the conditions that are reported to show improvement with the consumption of Colloidal Gold are:

Arthritis, Brain Dysfunction, Cancer, Chills, Circulatory Disorders, Depression, Digestive Disorders, Addiction, Gland Dysfunction, Hot Flashes, Insomnia, Joint Inflammation, Night Sweats, Obesity, Seasonal Affective Disorder (SAD).

Gold is an element of the treatments in the Edgar Cayce readings, especially those with glandular and nervous system disorders. These disorders range from multiple sclerosis and rheumatoid arthritis to Alzheimer's disease and depression. Cayce is the American super-psychic and father of the modern human potential field. He is the primary influencer in hypnotherapy and even alternative histories of Atlantis and Ancient Egypt on some of the most eminent researchers today. But let's take a closer look…

In 1988, David Hudson filed a British patent that outlined the procedure for producing a new form of the transition metals (T-metals) called Orbitally Rearranged Monatomic Elements (ORMEs). The inventor suggested that this material, which appears as a fine white powder, represents a monatomic form of the T-metals, in which the electronic (and perhaps even the nuclear) orbitals are rearranged.

> *"Monatomic Elements are usually recognized as precious metals such as gold, silver, platinum, rhodium, iridium and others, which occur as molecules of their individual element state as more than one atom linked together. For example, gold in it's metal form is composed of six atoms linked together, while in its other form, there is only one atom existing at a time.*
>
> *The theory that David Hudson puts forth is that when these elements - normally recognised as metals - exist as only one atom at a time in their non-metal state, they exhibit super-conductive properties. This means that when electricity currents*

flow through these elements, there is virtually no impedance to this flow.

The problem is that there is no way, according to Mr. Hudson, that modern electrical technology can even detect elements that have super-conductive properties, which is because the instrumentation is fooled by the super-conductivity in the different monatomic elements.

According to Mr. Hudson, gold miners have been fascinated by a substance called white gold, which are the tailings (sludge) left over after gold recovery from the earth. Many people have tried to find a way to extract the mysterious substance in tailings in large quantities but have failed so far.

Based on analysis, these tailings have always exhibited the strange property of not being capable of analysis - they have been classified as substances unknown by testing labs.

As it turns out, monatomic elements also have substantial healing properties. These elements exist in the body, particularly in the nervous system. Many plants contain monatomic elements as well, interwoven within the botanical molecules. According to some research, the more people can increase the amount of these super-conductive elements in their body, the greater the body's capacity is to heal itself.

The immune system is nothing more than a communication system, and by increasing the speed and efficiency of cell-to-cell communication; the body can then more easily identify and eliminate disease.

Another hypothesis is that monatomic elements also clear distortions in the DNA molecule – from the ground floor of biochemical function in the body, there is a clearing of any health issues and disease tendencies.

The cells communicate with each other not only with chemicals and electrically via the nervous system, but also via photons. A lack of photons in the cells, as well as needing to be organised correctly, will inhibit the capacity of the immune system to be able to recognize and eliminate disease. Monatomic elements seem to increase the level of photons in the cells, as well as reorganizing their active function to promote health."

— DR. DAVID WHEELER

It is suggested that Monatomic Gold increases transformation and manifestation in the following:

- Restoration of Youth and Vitality.
- Activates the Pineal Gland and Third Eye.
- Opens Gateway to the Next Dimension/s/ and Source Codes Gateway.
- Instant Manifestation of Thought.
- Lifts the Veil of Lives and Incarnations.
- Activates Extraordinary Knowingness and Awareness.
- Enables Levitation.
- Enables Ascension.

So what does this all have to do with the Neturu of Ancient Egypt? This links back into AKHU and the template of Cosmic Man. Hudson calls them "ORMES" for 'Orbitally Rearranged Monatomic Elements'.

This is a new form of matter with entirely different physical properties from normal elements. The white powder has a fluorescent-like glow again linking us back to the descriptions of The Shining Ones. It is possible that these elements generate a subtle energetic force that illuminates the body and energy system, just as in earlier descriptions of The Shining Ones.

This force may be viewed as the subtle energy field that links consciousness and body known as Holy Spirit, prana, chi, or life force. It was also called Amrita Rasa, the nectar of immortality. The action of ORMES elements may cause the fluid of empty space to transform itself into the nectar of immortality that explains the incredible life span of The Shining Ones and the eternity of Osiris.

Modern science tells us that all matter in the Universe is in a state of rotation. Stars rotate around the centre of galaxies, planets rotate around stars, and planets rotate on their own axes. All these celestial systems may be understood as cosmic mechanisms and cycles to generate life force from the vacuum that is also described in the Heliopolis Creation Myth. This process may also be interpreted on a microscopic scale. Subatomic particles spin around the centre of the atom trillions of times per second. Awakening, activating and maintaining life force at cellular level can master highest spiritual intelligence.

I believe this is what the Ancient Egyptians understood, achieved and harnessed within themselves to manifest as living gods. I believe this is what is hidden from us today. The Gold of Gods, Hathor, is the force that underpins creation, ancient super-knowledge and technologies that bend time and create the cosmic template of man.

CHAPTER 6

Couture Shamanism –
Travelling into
Super-Technologies

C entral to all worldwide shamanistic practices are experiences of other dimensions and levels of understanding profoundly different from conventional low-frequency awareness. Only through exact knowledge, frequencies and gateways can the initiated and trained shaman become the highly skilled mediator between ordinary and multi-dimensional realities, to open the door or climb the ladder of ascension with others.

Shamanic themes involve initiatory and ritualistic death processes, trance states, dismemberment, rebirth, renewal, shape-shifting, miracles of knowledge and healing, mystical and visionary experiences, lucid dreaming, astral travelling and 'out of body' experiences. The trained shaman can enter direct communication with ancestors, deities, many realities and dimensions. These themes are found in Ancient Egypt.

In Ancient Egypt, magician, priest, healer, priestess and pharaoh fulfilled the traditional role of shaman. Even Plato (428/427 or 424/423 BCE– 348/347 BCE) spent thirteen years learning with the ancient Egyptian priest, Sechnuphis. Here we have a very different shamanic template than in tribal shamanism. Here is the cosmic template of man and the technologies of cosmic man. This is what super-excites when exploring Ancient Egypt. This is the template for the super-dynasties that declined after Akhenaton and Tutankhamun.

AKHU AS THE ARCHETYPAL COSMIC MAN is central to Ancient Egypt. Akhu is found in Hermetic and Gnostic teachings. Osiris is central to the shamanic themes of death and rebirth processes. Osiris connects us with initiatory rites into the myths of death, resurrection and rebirth. Every pharaoh was regarded as the living Horus and upon death, the living Osiris. The Sed Festival is linked with the thirty-year cycle – an important renewal of kingship and youth.

During The Sed Festival food offerings are trampled by oxen and then removed by asses. This is symbolic of Seth's subordination to Osiris. The rising of the Djed Pillar signifies the demize of the force of Seth, followed by further offerings presented as the 'Eye of Horus'. The shen ring as the ring of eternity or crown with two feathers is used in the coronation of the pharaoh.

This link takes us to the descriptions of The Shining Ones. The priests chant to the 'Eye of Horus' as the king eats the sacred offerings as the AKHU. The Akhu is indistinguishable from Horus and Osiris. This is a fascinating infinite process of alchemy and rejuvenation. The secret rites of The Sed Festival were first held in pyramids. This links us once again with the purpose of the Great Pyramids complex. The Pyramid Texts refer to the ladder or Djed Pillar as one of the modes of ascent for the king. The images of this ladder and transformation into a bird also features. The mystical ladders of the Orphic Mysteries symbolize the ascent to heaven.

The root is shamanic – the sky ladder was importantly created by Ra and Horus, Utterance 306 of The Pyramid Texts, and links heaven and earth, in Utterance 307 of The Pyramid Texts. The Bull of Heliopolis, the solar bull known as the Mnevis Bull of Heliopolis symbolizes inexhaustible creativity of Source, Ra.

Once again we have connection with The Shining Ones. The Pyramid Texts are some of the earliest known religious texts in the world, reserved only for the pharaoh; the date recorded is estimated between ca. 2400–2300 BC by Allen, James, in *The Ancient Egyptian Pyramid Texts*.

The passages, inscribed on the subterranean walls of the pyramid of King Unas at Saqqara, reveal that the Egyptians enlisted the magical assistance of Semitic Canaanites from the ancient city of Byblos, located in modern Lebanon. Moshe Bar-Asher is a Hebrew professor at the Hebrew University and president of the Academy of the Hebrew Language, in 2010. This is what Bar-Asher said:

> *"This is a discovery of utmost importance. Almost all the words found are also found in the Bible."*

This is fascinating evidence in our quest to discover truths of Ancient Egypt that have been omitted. After some 180 years post ca. 2400–2300 BC, The Pyramid Texts were no longer in original use and yet they provide some fascinating insights of advanced ascension technologies in pyramids. But why disregard these truths if they link advanced consciousness and advanced technologies so brilliantly?

Let's fast–forward into the Eighteenth Dynasty, the reign of Amenhotep III and to his Sed Festival. In the tomb of Queen Teye's chief steward, Kheruef, who administered her estates and wealth, a scene of Hathor and King enthroned, is depicted. This tomb is close to Hateshepsut's Temple. In this scene, between Hathor and king is Queen Teye, in solar splendour, with two cobras with the crowns of Upper and Lower Egypt. A uraei surrounds her head. She is wearing a horned headdress with plumes. Teye is the Egyptian Queen of serpent power.

This Queen is also Akhenaton's mother and Tutankhamun's likely grandmother! Yet this serpent power is buried in history. The triad of King, Queen and Hathor replenishes the King's power and youth. Note here youth and the connection with The Shining One's ability to transform life span. The King must enter the Netherworld (or *neter world*) and with him, the whole of Egypt regains power.

Hathor 'Gold' is called upon as the Snake Goddess of the night to implore her to take the king to the east of the sky to be re-born. Hathor 'Gold' initiates him into new existence only in the east at dawn. Hathor's musical and mercurial child, Ihy is symbolized as a bull calf. As child of Hathor, Ihy is known as the child of gold, connected with renewal in the solar cycle.

In the Book of the Dead, chapter, 109, the vignette shows a young bull calf before Ra-Horakhti as helper for rebirth in the east. (Linking with the Israelites during The Exodus from Egypt.) As an incarnation of Maat, the royal Queen Teye, plays an important role in the rebirth of King. She is described as '*like Maat in the following of Re*'. The Maat principle depicts truth, justice, and morality.

If united with Hathor, Maat is the principal who guides, in beauty and magnificence. Here, the queen orchestrates and controls the force of Hathor to bring new life at dawn. Hathor is known as the Patroness of Serâbit el Khâdim. Hathor is solar deity tied to House of Gold, goddess and force of sexual love, beauty and music. Hathor is known in one of the earliest records, Narmer Palette. The only Goddess depicted in full face.

Hathor is known as

- Female Hawk
- Cow of Gold
- Lady of The Sycamore Tree
- Great Lady of Punt (Patroness of incense, gold and myrrh.)
- A venomous cobra breathing fire against the king's enemies.

Hathor is also known in this story when Ra opened his eyes inside the lotus as it emerged from the primordial chaos and his eyes began to weep, and droplets fell to the ground. They were transformed into a beautiful woman who was named Gold of the Gods, 'Hathor the Great, Mistress of Denderah'.

The Osirion Myth

According to Plutarch, during the absence of Osiris from Egypt, wife and consort Isis maintained control but upon his return, Seth plotted against Osiris and formed a group of conspirators. Seth had the cooperation of a Queen from Ethiopia called Aso (the personification of the burning winds of the South). Seth secretly measured Osiris' body and made a chest corresponding to size.

During festivities, the chest was presented and promised to the man who exactly fitted it. Of course, no one but Osiris fitted the chest. The lid was slammed shut, Osiris was trapped and the chest was sent far away to sea. Osiris was twenty-eight years old (note here the link with the 28 day lunar cycle). Isis wandered everywhere to discover the fate of Osiris. As she reached the Taniatic Mouth, she discovered the chest had been cast down at Byblos.

Isis travelled on to Byblos. Here, she transformed into a swallow that hovered around the pillar where the chest was concealed. The King and Queen granted that the chest should be removed. Isis removed the chest to the desert nearby but Seth discovered it, opened it and cut the body of Osiris into 14 pieces, scattering the parts throughout Egypt.

In each nome of Egypt a serapeum was built for one of those pieces. The only part Isis did not recover was his penis. This she created in gold. Osiris was restored and he went on to train Horus, his son, for combat with Seth to protect Egypt. *Please note here the power of the feminine in miracles of restoration and rejuvenation.*

The Shining Ones

Christian O'Brien and Joy O'Brien, in *The Genius of The Few, The Story of Those who Found the Garden of Eden,* describe The Shining Ones as a group of culturally and technically super-advanced people who settled and established an agricultural and teaching epicentre, estimated 9300–8200 BC.

So what does the science of the pineal gland have to do with The Shining Ones? Could it be the key to understanding outstanding health that upgrades human intelligence redesigning our technologies and world to the next level? At around 5500 BC, The Shining Ones dispersed from The Garden of Eden or Kharsag for Egypt, Western Europe, Scandinavia, Britain, Ireland, France, Italy, Greece, Crete, Cyprus, China, Asia and Japan.

The O'Briens go on to suggest the site of the Garden of Eden to be in Rachaiya Basin South, 8 miles (12 kms) north of Mt Hermon in Lebanon (Latitude) 33o 30' 4" N Long (DMS) 35o 50' 22"E. This valley lies above the Bekaa Plateau on the Anti-Lebanon Mountains near the Jabal Ash-Shakh (Mount Hermon) range.

This Ennead of Nine comprises of The Most High, the Lord of The Spirits and Seven Archangels. This nine-fold pantheon of God links with The Gread Ennead of Heliopolis, Egypt, which was known as On. Northeast of the Great Pyramids complex of Giza, during Pharaonic Egyptian times, Heliopolis stood as the pinnacle of higher learning of Egypt of the whole ancient world of the time.

Heliopolis was the centre of Astronomy, Geometry, Medicine, History, and Philosophy. The high priests of Heliopolis were called 'Chief of Observers' or 'Greatest of Seers'. This obviously takes us into exploring super-awareness. During my journeys in Japan, I have made links to a living legacy of The Shining Ones in Japan. Contemporary Shintoism is known as 'kami no michi' which is translated as the way of the Gods and upheld by the Imperial Family.

Amateresu-ōmikami is worshipped as the primary solar deity and is translated as 'shining in heaven'. The Ise Jingu, Japan's Shinto primary temple complex is indeed created in the template of The Garden of Eden. Here is a link between the helical rising of Sirius and the Summer Solstice (June 21-22). Sirius rises and shines in the night sky once again. Sirius is connected with Isis and Hathor in the rising of the Nile waters at this time. Amateresu-ōmikami can be linked as the archetypal earth mother with Isis of Egypt and Ninkharsag of The Shining Ones.

It is fascinating to further note, when I visited The Kanayama Megaliths, Gifu Prefecture – that this is the first site in Japan that has conducted a systematic archaeoastronomical investigation. Important connections with the ancient Egyptian Sothic Calendar and the helical rising of Sirius are being documented and research assisted by an American university.

The Shining Ones acknowledged two remarkable trees, the tree of life and the tree of understanding. Could it be here, that this is the key for understanding health, well-being and the extended life span of The Shining Ones? Just like the Shem Shu Hor, The Shining Ones were outstanding specialists in geology, anthropology and *astronomy*. The Shining Ones are also the seven foot tall Watchers, the source of global legends and mythologies of ancient giants.

During the pre-dynastic period, c.5500 BC, Osiris as an Anannage Lord (or Shining One) travelled to Egypt with three other Lords; Thoth, Anubis and Upant. In Ancient Egypt, the spiritual and agricultural traditions of men were developed and cared for by Osiris and Isis for four millennia. Here there is such a close correlation with Enlil and Ninlil of the Garden of Eden (Kharsag). The Serperia were also known as Senior Shining Ones.

The awakened kundalini is the divine force triggered at the base of the spinal column, sequentially through each chakra to the crown. Here the yogi or shaman is in union with the supreme universal soul. The initiated Shining Ones were described as shining with fiery eyes. The activation of the pineal and crown chakra is absolutely key in returning to the magnificence of our ancient past. Their word GURISH is sage, and our modern word guru comes from this root. Ninlil is the archetype of all mothers and goddesses globally.

Could it be that these angels were incredible advanced beings of humanity that later became a source of a global and universal mythology?

EL	(Sumerian)	- Shining
ILU	(Akkaden)	- Bright One
ELLU	(Babylon)	- Shining One
ELLYC	(Old Welsh)	- Shining Being
AILLIL	(Old Irish)	- Shining
EL	(Old Cornish)	- Angel
EL	(Hebrew)	- The Shining One

ANG-EL: Useful further Information

- ANGELS in this 'Garden of Eden' are known as One Eyed Serpents; Anannage, Elohim, en-ge-li, Lords of the Cultivation, (and associated with ap-kar-lu, genie, djinne, djoune, mal'ak, ha'neshim, tuatha de danann, serpents, and druids across the globe).
- SEVEN ARCHANGELS are often known as Two Eyed Serpents, Anannage Council, Elohim, Senior Teachers.
- ARCHANG-EL GABRIEL is known as Governor of Kharsag, Ninlil/Ninkharsag, Inanna, Bel, it, Isis, Neith, Mama, Kali, Ka, Coatlicue, Serpent Lady, Queen of Heaven and all Earth Mother archetypes.
- ARCHANG-EL URIEL is Lord of the Land, Enki.
- ARCHANG-EL RAGUEL is Lord of Sun Wisdom and Law, Utu, Ugmash, Shamash, Ogimus, Ogma, Og.
- ARCHANG-EL MICHAEL is Captain of the Guard.
- ARCHANG-EL RAPHAEL is Chief Medical Officer.
- ARCHANG-EL SARIEL is Representative of the Watchers.
- ARCHANG-EL REMIEL is Supervisor of Instructions.
- THE MOST HIGH is Supreme Commander of Anannage or Leader of The Shining Ones, Yahweh Elohim (associated with An, Anu, Ptah, Nawu, Ukqili, Bunjil, Puluga, Allah, Amun, Amen, Baal, Baal Hadad, Bel, Manu, Manitu, Manco Copac, El Shaddai, El Elyon, Quetzalcoatl across the globe).

- The Lord of the Spirits is the LORD OF CULTIVATION. Enlil is also known as OSIRIS. The Anunnage were known as The People of the Plough.

Yahweh connects this story with Akhenaton and the even earlier depiction of Aten and Ra. Yahweh, a Shining One was depicted in the Hebrew chronicles of the Flight from Egypt around 1200 BC, to the collapse of the Babylonian Empire in 539 BC. The O'Briens suggest, through their extensive study, that the Hebrew nation was achieved by a process of selection and can be traced to the Garden of Eden and Noah.

Yahweh's move of his 'Chosen People' can be traced to Terah, father of Abraham, who lived in Ur of the Chaldeans, Ancient Sumer, and relocated to Haran around 2000 BC. Abraham's family were also selected. Please note here the extensive life span of The Shining Ones, which would make this possible. This pattern of intervention brought the aged Abraham and Sarah, a son. Yahweh carefully monitored this lineage that went on to develop over five hundred years in Egypt, until The Exodus.

In *The Book of Enoch*, Enoch documents The Shining Ones. Dr R.H. Charles, a fellow of Merton College, Oxford, translated *The Books of Enoch*. This piece of history is fascinating. Around 325 AD, *The Book of Enoch* fell into disuse and was lost for almost one thousand five hundred years until it was discovered in Ethiopia. The Book of Enoch gives the bibliographical account of Enoch's experience living and working with The Shining Ones in The Garden of Eden.

This is an account of a super-age, a golden age of immense technological advancement that had already occurred in our ancient past. The Arc Covenant was positioned in the Great Tent of Yahweh, later becoming the template for shrines and temples throughout the Semitic world, which culminated in the Temple of Solomon in Jerusalem. Yahweh is described as at least 2.4 metres to 4 metres tall. The Ariel craft over the Tent of Yahweh is described in detail and reminds us of the Eye of Horus as described in *The Contendings of Horus and Seth*.

> *'And so it was a stately Being – his clothes shone more brightly than the sun, and whiter than any snow. None of the Angels was allowed to enter the room, and none of the honoured attendants could look on his face; no flesh could bear it. The blazing light was all around him and no-one could approach him.'*
>
> — *EN XIV:9-25 PP*

Another passage of the Israelite chroniclers reads:

> *'Moses made a copper serpent and mounted it on a standard (staff). And if anyone who is bitten looks at it, he shall recover.'*
>
> — *NUM 21:4-9 TH VB*

This connects beautifully with the symbol of caduceus that is a powerful symbol of modern medicine and healing.

Heliopolis

> *'O you Great Ennead which is Ōn(Heliopolis), Atum, Shu, Tefēnet, Gēb, Nūt, Osiris, Isis, Seth, and Nephthys; O you children of Atum, extend his goodwill to his child in your name of Nine Bows.'*
>
> — *THE PYRAMID TEXTS,* **1665 PT**

So what is the connection with the solar cult of Ra, The Shining Ones and our final pharaoh Akhenaton? What is the connection with Abu Ghorab and Heliopolis? The Benben stone is pyramidal in form. This prototype at Heliopolis inspired all future obelisks of Ancient Egypt. The original 'Mansion of the Phoenix' is the original temple where the Benben stone was housed at Heliopolis.

This is linked with cosmic cycles and world ages associated with the Precession of the Equinoxes. This knowledge and legacy was passed down by the gods through the Creation Myth of Heliopolis and what the Ancient Egyptians regarded as the First Time, *'Zep Tepi'*, an ancient, ancient time when the neturu lived on earth. The neteru is the living legacy of The Shining Ones.

As 'the Complete One' and 'The Not Yet Existent One', Atum rises from the water upon the primordial mound to create the first cosmic pair, neteru, Shu and Tefnut. A realm of radiant light is created. Khepri 'he who becomes' appears in the east horizon. The cosmos begins to unfold, the sky goddess, Nut and earth god, Geb are born to Shu and Tefnut. The separation of Geb and Nut is complete so that Osiris, Isis, Seth and Nephtys can be born from the celestial womb.

It is fascinating to note Alison Robert's research and the presence of the goddesses of attraction that rouse the androgynous creator, Atum. The Heliopolitan goddesses were powerful partners of Atum and, later, were often deliberately deleted from The Creation Myth account. These goddesses are Iusaas and Nebet Hetepet, associated with Hathor. This is again evidence that the archetypal mother is essential in the Creation Myth. There would be neither cosmos nor seed without the presence of these goddesses, representing Mother and Daughter. This duality brings life into being from darkness into light, and existence from primordial beginnings. This critical template has been deliberately deleted.

This is also a critical template in spirituality, peace and evolution in modern times.

The Great Ennead of Heliopolis comprises of Atum, Shu, Tefnut, Nut, Geb, Osiris, Isis, Seth and Nephtys. The Benben Stone at Heliopolis, whose origin is rooted in Atum, takes us closer to the source of creation.

Even Akhenaton named his solar temple at Karnak, 'the Mansion of the Benben Stone' linking this pharaoh with the knowledge and initiation rites of The Shining Ones. The journey to Ra is only through the divine feminine.

This is the journey to The Source Codes. This is the route to understand and experience new higher frequency templates of evolution and change beyond the prolonged mode of conflict and survival that is experienced by almost every individual on this planet.

> *Atum-Khepri,*
> *you are high on the hill,*
> *You shine forth as Benben,*
> *In the Benben Temple of Heliopolis,*
> *You eject Shu. You spit out Tefnut,*
> *You put your arms around them with your ka,*
> *So that your ka is in them.*
>
> — *THE PYRAMID TEXTS* 1652-3

The Priests of Heliopolis, The Shem Shu Hor

The Priests of Heliopolis, Ancient Egypt were also super-proficient in prophecy, astronomy, mathematics, architecture, magic and arts just like The Shining Ones. *The Benben stone is linked with the reality eternity and the Philosopher's Stone.* The Philosopher's Stone links us with Akhu, this is the template of Cosmic Christ within man.

This is a very exciting Source Codes template to discover and activate to upscale modern living. Not only the story but the essential life changing, world changing high frequency! Here are some further fascinating links.

- **AKHU** is the Cosmic Christ Template.
- **AKHA** is the name of Ancient Egypt's First Dynasty Kings. This is super-exciting! Take a look at the preceding history of Christ. The Stone

of Palmero lists 120 kings who preceded the First Dynasty (c. 2920 BC) describing The Amazaghen Kings as rulers of The House of Wadjet or Ouajet. Wadjet is the symbol of The Eye of Horus. Wadj has its origins in Osirion legends as we have earlier explored. The Djedu or Pillar People were pre-dynastic shepherd tribes who inhabited the town of Djedu (later Bursitis).This later became Per Usire or House of Osiris.

- **HER OR HORUS** is symbolized in the icon of the hawk with raised wings. This is also a powerful source of Ancient Egyptian Pharaonic rule. *HER evolves to the later HORUS and can be translated as SHINING. HORUS IS THE IMPORTANT SYMBOL OF LIGHT AND SHINING BRILLIANCE. THIS CREATES A LIVING LINEAGE TO THE SHINING ONES WITHIN US. YOUR LIGHT AND BRIL-LIANCE.* This links you with the oldest of archaic cults.

- The Atef is a ram's horn crown, crowning Osiris as an icon of immortality and eternity in the inner shrine of MAAT. MAAT is synonymous with truth, justice and cosmic order. Here in the Land of Dreams is the gateway to divine feminine wisdom. MAAU-TAUI encompasses all the neteru – *THE SOURCE CODES*.

- Two lions guard this inner sanctuary, one is the lion of yesterday and one is the lion of tomorrow. This MAAT PRINCIPLE governs the ladder or journey of a greater humanity and world. You may know or have read about this ladder but are you granted entrance? Understanding this principle for entry is key for super-consciousness and super-change.

- It is fascinating to also note here, HORUS is 'The Lord of Djeba', 'The Blood of Neith' and 'The House of Dadu'. The Djed Pillar in The Sed Festival is also known as the pillar of immortality and eternity. The icon of HORUS lands on the Djed and guards The Pillar of Eternity. *THIS IS THE MISSING KNOWLEDGE OF ETERNITY AND DIVINITY.* This reminds us of the purpose of The Sphinx and the role of the Great Pyramids Complex.

- **AKH-AKH** is the region of the stars regarded by The Amazigh who are the indigenous peoples of North Africa often regarded as Libyco-Berber. AKHU are the venerated ancestors of the Amazigh. This primordial root is AKH. AKH can also be translated as spirit. ANKH can be derived from AKH. This links us with celestial origins that take us on a journey exploring a cosmic template of man. With this in mind, we can super-upscale magnificence. How exciting is that! So much of this evidence is pointing the way to creating a new story!

CHAPTER 7

Time Travelling
is Now Possible

As I walk through the enchanting muddle of personalities, colours, camels and horses, I finally sit, quietly alone, in the cool winter sun. This vast landscape is a time machine. I sit on the west side of The Great Pyramid. Pyramid Khafre is a short walk in the distance. I sit, melting my back into the deep baseline of limestone blocks. I run my awareness from the base to the apex of the pyramid, checking the frequency and the history, the templates and the stories. The next template of humanity is indicated by the precession of the equinox.

I can vision the world today; The Great Pyramid has recorded the history of man at this time. The healing required is visibly mirrored in the lower structure. The next template depicts time finally catching up and evolution accelerates at incredible speeds. This is the vision to come. Here two incredible opposing stories of humanity collide. As the next template sits in this exact time machine, I have visions of how this cosmic template of man has been deliberately hidden and deleted by the stories of elite power structures.

How this gigantic, infinite and peaceful template for world has been deliberately withheld. Deliberately manipulated, reality now depicts a world in deep need of a millennia of emotional healing and awakening. The limited template of humanity has driven, monopolized and controlled illusion, love, money, control and even our divine power. This is the ultimate free resource for changing self and our world.

I recall many experiences in my life when I have experienced great challenges. There is a deep and emotional narrative here today within me that reflects the same story of humanity. And today emotion heals me. The vision of a greater template washes over me as I sink deeply into The Great Pyramid and surrender. This is the only way to freedom.

This time machine has recorded the path of humanity and has been designed to amplify this cycle of the Precession of the Equinox to accelerate and awaken a better path. Secrets of time and whispering memories of a powerful ancient humanity are held here. What has happened? The Great Time Machine records the history of our times and where we have travelled. The information is encrypted here. The

Great Time Machine is filtering and transforming earth and humanity. Our collective stories could be changed faster if we understood how this technology works.

The ancients left incredible solutions for our modern times. As I recognize this legacy high frequency intensifies. Awareness of greater truths intensifies. My heart is awakened and I am flying. Held in the all seeing eye of Ra. Planetary evolution is building to unlock the apex of The Great Pyramid; the benben stone, the symbol of the phoenix, is the next template of humanity. This is the big and long awaited change. Divinity reveals awareness and awareness heals and yet still the old template stubbornly exists.

The Great Time Machine indicates the purpose behind this. Physicality, the challenges of life and the deliberate limitations on the template of humanity serve as a counter balance, anchoring the way to propel us into the new template at incredible speed. This template knows and accepts who we have been and the history we have created so far. This cosmic template recognizes the mistakes of our past and heals the deliberately incomplete history and vision for self and humanity.

And now The Great Pyramid also records the story of the incredible sea of children who run to me and welcome me. One hundred children surround me, passionately talking with me and taking photos. Enchanting, they inspire their teachers to talk with me and the walls of adult silence are broken easily. I am held in a frenzy of stories of loving daily life. I break from writing, for time with these radiant, loving children. Here is the hope for the world right in front of me. There is love, so much unconditional love.

〜〜

The Sphinx is calling. Egypt has returned to a busy pre-evolution self. It is somewhat different; the modern generation of Egyptians is now discovering the ancient monuments for the first time. There is wild fascination and innocent hearts that permits entry to the unseen powerful cosmic template. I can see the pyramid complex alive and activated by this purity of heart and excited new experiences.

The few austere international tourists don't sparkle in the same way. This new generation is on fire, alive with love and dreams of a future in innocent hearts. The story is of hope and gratitude despite difficult years post-revolution. The Sphinx is designed to show the way of the hero, built majestically into the eastern heart of the Giza complex.

The path of the hero unlocks resource to power Khafre and ignite the feminine principle. I see the vast complex oscillating to maintain balance. Not one site is separate but is a vast, interconnected complex, inter-dependent. These deliberate clues are easily missed by narrow analysis and untrained vision. The knowledge here is multi-dimensional and powerfully inter-connected.

The Sphinx is the battery of eternity in this vast time machine. This power site opens the heart. I vision The Sphinx and an immense portal opening through the paws, heart and third eye to the east, to what now is Mecca. The Sphinx has been silenced and it is time to speak the secrets of our past. As the seat of the later Emerald Tablet, The Sphinx's eternal power shows the eternal spiritual way for humanity. The path of truth, of positive and good.

I sit quietly and patiently for this knowledge cannot be forced. I can feel the power of gravity and being alive. The lion of yesterday and the lion of tomorrow reveal the ancient origins of our future. This is the way of hyper-speed humanity that can power super-speed solutions to resolve the mistakes of our recent histories. Bending time....Egypt is fast resurrecting as the Phoenix to rebuild, and all is hope. The choice and way being made is resourceful, positive and good.

— NOVEMBER 2014.

In the Land of Dreams is the gateway to *MAAU-TAUI*. Maau-taui encompasses all the neteru – *THE SOURCE CODES*. Described as an inner sanctuary, two lions guard it, one is the lion of yesterday and one is the lion of tomorrow. The *MAAT PRINCIPLE* governs the ladder or journey of a greater humanity and world.

The Great Ennead of Heliopolis comprises of Atum, Shu, Tefnut, Nut, Geb, Osiris, Isis, Seth and Nephtys. In the Great Ennead of the Heliopolitan Creation Myth, Atum created Shu. Shu was consort to Tefnut, and produced Geb as earth god and Nut as sky deity. Shu separated these two deities after Nut swallowed the constellations.

Shu is also mentioned in The Pyramid Texts when the king is transformed in the 'lakes of Shu'. This deity is also connected with light and incorporated within aten. Aten is linked with eternity. Aten is also 'the Prince of Maat'. Shu is represented as a lion in the Maat-Taui holding the lions of yesterday and tomorrow.

It can be concluded that the principle of Shu will aid you in time travelling to past and future events. Teftnut is daughter of Atum. Tefnut is known as the creator of pure water. Tefnut is also depicted as a lion-headed serpent governing eternity. In the following information the *MAAT PRINCIPAL* explains how we can enter the Zero Point Field as The Pyramid Texts describes. In *The Field*, Lynn McTaggart writes about scientist Hal Puthoff, who received funding to develop an infinite energy source extracted from a vacuum.

Way back in 1973, Hal Puthoff, a brilliant laser physicist, began his search for alternatives to fossil fuels. His research objective: to improve the planet. He suggested manipulating the Zero Point Field in this quest to discover and harness alternative fuels. This void is active. Heisenberg had developed the uncertainty principle; here no particle stayed at rest.

The sub-structure of the universe is a sea of quantum fields. The vacuum or Zero Point Field is a matrix of infinite energy resource or light. A field is a matrix connecting two points in space. There is emission and reabsorption with all quantum particles. The Zero Point field is the matrix where all matter is interconnected by waves through space. *This is a dynamic equilibrium – zero point energy (The Source Codes) connects all matter in the universe and is the key for time travelling.*

This is fascinating when we have already considered the neutral point in the kundalini force as the key to entering The Source Codes. This is the very special key of time travelling, accelerating transformation and awakening, and entry to the records of information (ancient and future). Waves are encrypted with information. These subatomic waves imprint the infinite record of the universe, time and no time, the beginning and the end.

Time travelling literally means riding or travelling those waves to enter the matrix and the record of all time. Not only this, Hal Puthoff, also knew that levitation and psychokinesis was entirely possible if gravity could be manipulated. If matter was not stable then just as described in the ladder of ascension in The Pyramid Texts and shamanism traditions worldwide, entry could lead to other fields and other information.

If we know how to gain entry we can tap into a vast energy and unconventional structures of information that defy time and conventional reality. This has been the domain of mystics and yogis, seers and visionaries, miracle healers and saints.

It is a scientific, mystical and spiritual reality that we might all utilize to bend time and shape reality and future. Just like Hal Puthoff – to improve the planet and humanity by accessing the matrix for powerful, positive vision and responsible solutions in the world we live in today. What is fascinating is that the limits of modern consciousness are not currently configured to enter and manifest at the level of the Source Codes or the Zero Point Field.

Only powerful initiation rites, kundalini processes and advanced spiritual awakening can unlock this entry, resource and super-information possibilities. As I said above, this is the realm of powerful mystics, shamans and yogis. Did the Ancient Egyptians leave clues to confirm and redefine consciousness? Is this what The Shining Ones knew and shaped reality and time in as super-gods? *If this is possible, then super-living becomes possible in The Source Codes.*

In 'Backing the Big Bang', Alvin Powell in *The Harvard Gazette*, 17 March 2014, writes:

> *'A telescope in the South Pole observing traces of the Big Bang that created the universe has turned up the first evidence of a key moment in that process: the blink-of-an-eye expansion of the universe from a dot into a vast soup of energy and particles. The discovery, using the BICEP2 telescope at the Amundsen-Scott South Pole Station, provided the first strong evidence of "cosmic inflation," which scientists say occurred in a fraction of the first second of the universe's existence, when it expanded billions of times over. MIT scientist Alan Guth first proposed the process in 1981.*
>
> *The expansion occurred during the inflationary epoch, which saw the fabric of space time itself grow in volume 10^{78} times in a process so rapid and energetic that it sent gravity waves rippling through the fabric of space time, to be detected by the BICEP2 team almost 14 billion years later.'*

And so the Ancients understood this knowledge that took scientists until 2014 to finally detect? This knowledge and legacy was passed down by the gods through the Creation Myth of Heliopolis and what the Ancient Egyptians regarded as the First Time, 'Zep Tepi'; the ancient time when the neteru lived on earth.

The neteru is the living legacy of The Shining Ones. As 'the Complete One' and 'The Not yet Existent One', Atum rises from the waters upon the primordial mound to create the first cosmic pair, neteru, Shu and Tefnut. A realm of radiant light is created. Khepri 'he who becomes' appears in the east horizon. The cosmos begins to unfold, the sky goddess, Nut and earth god, Geb are born to Shu and Tefnut. The separation of Geb and Nut is complete so that Osiris, Isis, Seth and Nephtys can be born from the celestial womb.

And guess what, there is more. 'In *'Water, Water Everywhere, Radio telescope finds water is common in universe'* Lee Simmons writes in *The Harvard Gazette* in 1999:

> *'The universe, it seems, is full of water. That's the message being beamed to Earth from a new space-based radio telescope. Launched into orbit on Dec. 5, 1998, the Submillimeter-Wave*

Astronomy Satellite (SWAS) is for the first time, detecting vast amounts of water vapor hidden in the dark pockets of our galaxy. The findings confirm what astronomers suspected, but have been unable to prove from the ground.'

'It's very gratifying,' says Gary Melnick of the Harvard-Smithsonian Centre for Astrophysics (CfA), who heads the scientific team behind the effort. "After 20 years of guessing that nature might work this way, to finally get an instrument up into space, turn it on, point it toward these regions and see confirmation – we're seeing water everywhere we look.'

And the very exciting relevant signs of contact have been recorded back in the 1970s! The Wow! signal was a strong narrow band radio signal detected by Jerry R. Ehman on August 15, 1977, while he was working on a SETI project at the Big Earradio telescope of The Ohio State University, then located at Ohio Wesleyan University's Perkins Observatory in Delaware, Ohio.

The signal bore the expected hallmarks of non-terrestrial and non-Solar System origin. It lasted for the full 72-second window that Big Ear was able to observe it, but has not been detected again. Ehman circled the signal on the computer printout and wrote the comment, 'Wow!' on its side. This comment became the legendary name of the signal.

The region of the sky lies in the constellation Sagittarius, roughly 2.5 degrees south of the fifth-magnitude star group Chi Sagittarii, and about 3.5 degrees south of the plane of the ecliptic. Tau Sagittarii is the closest easily visible star.

This is a scientific yes on life beyond earth. Of course we are not alone. And we are close to time travelling...

CHAPTER 8

The Denderah Zodiac

K nown as one of the oldest sacred places in Egypt, the first Temple of Hathor at Denderah was built during the Old Kingdom, during the reign of Khufu (2589–2566 BC). The present Temple of Hathor was built in the first century AD by Ptolemies.

When Denon first discovered the Temple of Hathor at Denderahin January 1799, he happened into a little stone chapel on the roof, where he found a large circular planisphere, or zodiac. Vivant Denon published the first drawing of the Zodiac in his *Voyage dans la Basse et la Haute Égypte* (Paris, 1802). The Zodiac was part of the ceiling of one of the chapels where the resurrection of Osiris was commemorated, on the roof of the great Temple of Hathor.

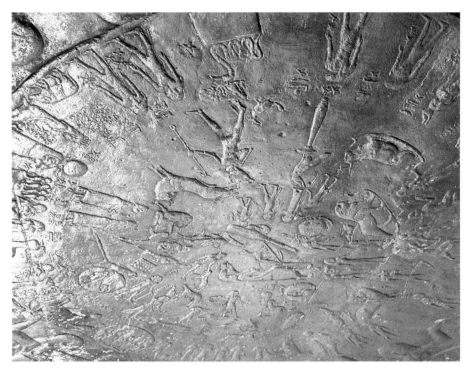

The Zodiac of Denderah.

Here, a disc, held up by four women assisted by falcon-headed spirits, represents the vault of heaven. The Denderah Zodiac is one of the most important surviving documents of antiquity. In 1822, Claude Lelorrain used explosives to remove the Zodiac; the original Denderah Zodiac is now in The Louvre, France.

The zodiac is a planisphere of the stars on a plane projection, showing the 12 constellations of the zodiacal band forming 36 decans of ten days each, and the planets. These decans are groups of first-magnitude stars. These were used in the ancient Egyptian calendar, which was based on lunar cycles of around 30 days and on the heliacal rising of the star Sothis (Sirius).

The Denderah Zodiac depicts Twelve zodiacs and the planets: Mercury, Venus, Mars, Jupiter, Saturn, the Moon, Sirius, Orion; the three known constellations of the north: Draco, Ursa Minor and Ursa Major, and the axis of the temple.

What is the Precession of the Equinoxes and why is it relevant in this story? The World Ages measured in the Zodiac provide the ultimate key of understanding to the evolutionary learning cycles of humanity. In Ancient Egypt, the day was divided into 24 hours, 12 hours of light and 12 hours of darkness. Each hour had a name specifying its force or influence. The months were of two kinds, lunar, 29 days and 30 days. Five days were consecrated to Osiris, Isis, Horus, Seth and Nephtys.

The Sothic Year is 365 1/4 days. The Sothic Year is linked with Sirius and the return to the heliacal rising of Sirius. This is the fixed year or 'year of God'. The heliacal rising of Sirius can be used to track all celestial movements. 1460 years completes the Sothic cycle. The heliacal rising of Sirius takes place one day earlier, each degree of latitude from North to South. This is a sliding gauge of time. The Ancient Egyptians had exceptional astronomical knowledge and the heliacal rising of Sirius celebrated the Festival of New Year.

The Pharaonic Sothic cycle of 1460 years records and predicts the summer solstice advancing 11.5 days in relation to the rising of Sirius. The Solstice gains 11 days per Sothic cycle and the return of the star loses 9 days. The vernal point is displaced by 20 days in 1460 days. The Precession of the Equinoxes is a cycle of 25,920 years. The vernal point travels through the twelve constellations.

Each twelve months is 2160 years and 3 decans of 720 years. We have also seen these measurements repeated in The Great Pyramid – also known as the 'House of God'. This is another nod to the next world phase and new template of cosmic man.

Horus and Seth

We must also look to the small, adjacent celestial observatory room just beyond The Denderah Zodiac for more clues on new world change. I have spent many hours working with meditation and transformation technologies at Denderah Temple to align with and understand the coming world age and the new technologies that accompany it. Perhaps the Osirion Mystery holds further clues.

Temple of Hathor, Denderah, 2011.

Seth enters the Creation Myth on day three hundred and sixty-five. This is the third day of the five epagomenal days added to the three hundred and sixty Egyptian civil calendar. On this day, Seth violently breaks out of the womb of Nut to create suffering to Osiris.

In 'The Contendings of Horus and Seth', Seth shows an insatiable appetite for women even with Isis, consort of Osiris. It has been suggested that these mythical events reflect actual events of pre-dynastic Egypt. Both the 'Eye of Horus' and the 'testicles' of Seth demonstrate similarities with Tibetan tantra involving light and semen. The 'Eye of Horus' is tied to the lunar cycle and restoration associated with the waxing moon. Isis and Hathor are also involved in this story.

Let's set the scene, in the court of The Ennead of Heliopolis presided over by Ra-Horakhti (the oldest of solar deities), where the judgement that Horus should succeed the throne of Egypt is given. Horus is son of Osiris and Isis. Re is displeased, considering Horus unfit. An alliance with Ra and Seth takes the Ennead into chaos.

At this point, it is the power of the feminine, the power of Hathor and Isis that intervenes to neutralize the anarchic forces of Ra and particularly, Seth. Hathor succeeds in restoring Re to the Ennead. In response, Seth attempts to claim his right to the throne as rightful protector of Ra. Seth cunningly persuades The Ennead to listen to the proceedings on the Island-In-The-Midst, without Isis.

It is useful to note that only Isis possesses the power to challenge Seth. Seth is now free to threaten and potentially remove all archaic tradition, custom and ancestry. The Shining Ones connection surfaces in this story as Isis has already created a snake from the mouth of Ra and extracted his secret name. This is critical as a serpent goddess and for power over Ra.

Isis, in the story, transforms and shape-shifts as mother, virgin and crone, often associated with universal lunar deities. As the crone, Isis is ferried to The Island-In-The-Midst where she once again transforms as a beautiful virgin whereupon Seth approaches her and is fooled into invalidating his claim to the throne.

The saga continues: Seth directs his ambitions upon Horus for a fight to prove himself king of Egypt. Horus and Seth, transform as two hippopotami and plunge into the deepest waters, locked in violent combat. Isis shoots and locks a harpoon into Seth. Seth as her brother (both Isis and Seth are children of Nut) appeals to release the harpoon. Horus is enraged and beheads Isis.

He flees to the desert, the domain of Seth, where Seth tears out the eyes of Horus. This episode ties with the loss of vision associated with young and gifted clairvoyant vision, often associated with initiates of shamanistic traditions. Here, Hathor returns to the story. The 'Eyes of Horus' are buried, transforming as lotus flowers.

The lotus flower is where Ra rises each morning. As 'Lady of the southern Sycamore' and the tree goddess of Memphis, she heals Horus with healing liquid, restoring Horus to the solar path, the path of light, the path of the hero back to Ra-Horakhti.

> 'I found Horus had lost his eyes because of Seth, but I restored them. Now here he comes.'

Isis is also transformed by Hathor; when she is given the cow's head, she is reconnected with Hathorian solar life from her restrictive maternal bonds with Horus. Horus returns to Ra-Horakhti. 'These powerful mythical narratives closely link with cult rites and shamanistic practices', *The Contendings of Horus and Seth* continue, and no longer weak, Horus is transformed and yet The Ennead has little patience.

The final contest between Seth and Horus involves Seth making sexual advances. Horus catches Seth's semen in his hand before taking it before Isis. Isis cuts off Horus' hand before creating a new one. The semen of Horus is collected in a jar. Isis places the content on Seth's garden, creating a cunning trap to plant the seed of Horus in Seth. At court, Seth begins by demanding the throne based upon his encounter with Horus. Horus requests that the sperm of Seth and Horus comes forward which it does. However, Seth has been tricked into becoming a container for the seed of Horus, and a lunar disc bursts from his head.

Thoth enters this story and claims the lunar disc as his own. The two oppositional forces of Seth and Horus are forced to concede or resolve. The re-emergence of light from Seth's head in the solar disc is the rebirth of the Eye of Horus, the Wedjat Eye.

The Eye has to be shattered to pieces to be made whole again. Seth now relinquishes his claim to the throne before Atum at Heliopolis. Horus unites Egypt in the Red Crown of Lower Egypt and White Crown of Upper Egypt. Of the two sacred 'Eyes', the left eye is 'Eye of Horus', connected with the waxing moon, and the right eye with the raging goddess Hathor-Sekhmet and ceremonial practices associated with this goddess. Hathor is Gold of The Gods, the cosmic template of woman.

Equinox Hopes

The Precession of The Equinoxes even brings hope that Earth will heal. This is written about in, *Earth's wobble 'fixes' dinner for marine organisms* by Catherine Zandonella, Office of the Dean for Research, Princeton University, September 13, 2013. She suggests that according to a new study in the journal Nature the cyclic wobble of the Earth controls a nutrient essential to the health of the ocean; this sheds light on the way the ocean regulates its life-support system, which again has implications on our climate and the size of fisheries. Researchers from Princeton University and the Swiss Institute of Technology in Zurich (ETH) have reported that the vacillations in nitrogen fixation, the essential nutrient to the health of the ocean, during the past 160,000 years closely follows a pattern matching the changing orientation of the Earth's axis of rotation.

This axial precession occurs on a cycle of approximately 26,000 years (the Precession of the Equinox). 1980's studies revealed that the precession sets in motion an upwelling of deep ocean water in the Atlantic Ocean every 23,000 years. Through this nitrogen-poor water rises to the surface; nitrogen from the air is then transformed by blue green algae in a form that is biologically usable. Considering this apparent correlation, Daniel Sigman, Professor of Geological and

Geophysical Sciences, Princeton University, suggests that the ocean biosphere can even recover during massive ecological changes.

Sirius

The gateways with Isis, Horus, Hathor and Osiris to the Sirius star system has brought incredible transformational experiences that have taken me closer to the cosmic heartbeat and understanding the nature of our existence.

The Source Codes are powerful frequency and information codes capable of shaping groundbreaking new realities. The Source Codes take us closer to greater intelligence, divinity and freedom beyond structures bound in unhealthy and corrupt hierarchies that constantly deny this level and freedom of sovereignty.

The Source Codes ultimately switch you on to the cosmic template. This level and freedom of sovereignty has been deliberately shut down for mass manipulation and control of our evolution. Even within our world of human potential that brings incredible hope, if our teachers and leaders, parents and friends are not awake, then the subtle stories controlling evolution frame our encounters and experiences in life again and again.

The only way is continuous self-work to freedom. Our spirituality is about choosing magnificent living and warrior-ship. It is measured by how we live, how we love and give generously in the world around us.

Sirius is the forgotten key of freedom. Sirius is the forgotten key of divinity. Beyond deliberately low-frequency, limited knowledge we need to experience a new profound high-frequency intelligence and peace that meditation may bring.

Beyond knowledge, we need super-energy resource for greater awareness and self-transformation that ignites essential contribution in the times we live in. The peace template is critical. The peace template is found in Sirius, in exploring the infinite cycles of archetypal stories of Isis, Osiris, Horus and Hathor and journeys explored here.

The obvious story on the walls of the adjacent room at Denderah is the transition of Osiris and Isis, to Horus and Hathor (this is recorded as the next world age in the Precession of the Equinoxes).

We can accelerate this transition in precision meditation and transformation, exploring, investigating and working with both. At this time, it is essential that you investigate during your meditation journeys to understand the next world age and what is required. This will help you to smooth into the next world age and into the next level of high frequency.

You will enter new frequencies and groundbreaking information unlike previous times. New frequencies and new information will help you shape a new future because it is now possible. Meditation practice can be used to further accelerate you and the possibilities of your life and world. Beyond knowledge, we need to succeed in greater love and vision to secure the future of our world and future generations. Beyond knowledge we need incredible awareness to continue healing and loving self and those we touch in our lives.

The next world age will redefine who we are and challenge what we have come to believe as truths. In exploring Sirius through meditation, an incredible sense of physicality, gigantic space and peace accelerates deep awareness to tackle and out-manoeuvre the subtle toxic stories often encountered in daily life. This takes us closer to tackling who we are and assimilating what and who we need in our lives, and what is healthy spiritually and what is not.

This constantly changes and requires attention to intelligently 'opt in' and 'opt out'. This quality of energy and information resource is outstanding and takes us some way towards grasping and creating the cosmic template of a new humanity that is the future of hope and healing despite challenging times. The constant cosmic cycle of evolution and renewal is the only reality.

When we enter this, we accelerate the meaning and potential of our existence and improve the world around us. The next world age does this. The next world age requires meticulous physicality with high-frequency intelligence and loving awareness that Sirius brings. This can ignite an absolute spirituality and transformation survival, and living, essential for sensitive individuals, indigos and spiritual warriors. Physicality and high-frequency emotional and intelligence spectrum go hand in hand with awakening the power of a new super-destiny that breaks down old structures and stories that often stand in the way of a more meaningful, loving existence on earth.

This is grown-up spirituality where awareness is key and intelligent decision-making is critical, in changing self and the world positively, to leave an old outdated world behind. In exploring Sirius, intelligence is awareness, infinite, vast and ever changing and this is the key to the next template of humanity. Awareness and transformation is richer, deeper and much more subtle where truths can be known on so many more yet undiscovered levels of potential and reality.

It is here in incredible new frontiers of meditation that we can be aware of the impact of our stories on the world around us and make an incredible difference not only to self but in the world around us every day. We can also use meditation to gain access to a new frontier of new possibilities and solutions for the world we live in today.

CHAPTER 9

Spiritual Warriorship
for Changing Times

In their groundbreaking book, *The Indigo Children*, Lee Carroll and Jan Tober describe the new generations of increasing numbers of children and adults that will create conscious and positive change. These generations encompass every age but the new Spiritual Warrior template is the same, designed to uphold evolution, humanity and earth as sacred.

These individuals have always been present in our world but it is now that this movement is increasing, awakening and powering to create the world change long overdue. Is this you?

> *'An Indigo Child is one who displays a new and unusual set of psychological attributes and shows a pattern of behaviour generally undocumented before. This pattern has unique factors that suggest those who interact with them change their treatment and upbringing of them in order to achieve balance. To ignore these new patterns is to potentially create imbalance and frustration in the mind of this precious life.'*
>
> — *LEE CAROL AND JAN TOBER,*
> **The Indigo Children**

The Indigo Children outlines the pre-cursor template of the current generations of change-makers and spiritual warriors who are throwing off toxic and non-evolutionary stories. Children and young adults do not only belong to this new wave of change-makers. The new spiritual warriorship template is present and growing in every generation, designed with razor-sharp awareness and spiritual power for positive change, exposing outdated structures and leading new frontiers of solutions.

This new template of spiritual warriorship is now urgently required beyond pain cycle agenda. The spiritual warrior is healed, loving and living mission and world. *Book Two helps you in igniting and maintaining the new higher fre-*

quency templates of change-maker, peace-maker, healer, spiritual warrior and visionary.

If you are ready to leave outdated and repeated pain cycles behind, if you are ready to live your dreams for earth and humanity, and if you are ready to lock into the high-frequency Source Codes templates, this is the perfect time to join the peaceful revolution to change the world, one individual at a time. And in every individual a global bond collaborates to create a better world.

As a conscious individual, parent or friend, the high-frequency template of individual and humanity must now be set free to deliver powerful, positive change that defies blatantly outdated yet difficult society structures, processes, elitism and ageism. It is time to tackle outdated structures easily and peacefully. You know it is the time, you feel it is the time for positive change.

Since 1999, I have chosen to work with new change-makers, spiritual warriors, peace-makers, world-healers, conscious individuals and indigos of all generations. I choose to help these individuals transform and power in magnificence to change the world. These individuals operate as incredible unique healers in all spheres of life. Their incredible vision and awareness of conscious and intelligent change is critical. Their incredible truth to move beyond outdated structures and low-frequency stories is the path of the hero. This is the path of true spirituality. *The journey that is truth. This is the path of one and a new global bond of spiritual warrior-ship that ties together unique and magnificent individuals of change. Individuals of all generations!*

Some of us are born spiritual warriors to power in the next phase of change and ignite the new templates for new stories of humanity and earth. Some of us have longed to empower all our lives to re-ignite the warrior template and manifest our dreams of conscious change.

I travel the globe sharing the knowledge of working with and empowering incredible individuals in every generation, not only children and young adults. I listen to their most magnificent stories to unlock their dreams of positive change. I teach them how to listen to and ignite their most magnificent stories beyond low-frequency stories that slow evolution and change.

Often these individuals have been pushed to conform in attempts made to hijack this incredible power. Often these individuals have not truly been respected or heard. I respect and hear them; their magnificence is restored.

When just one individual listens to your magnificent story it unlocks the incredible resource to ignite unique purpose and change. Every individual and story is non-generic with the potential to dazzle in magnificent purpose and resource to create positively in the world.

These are the times to live with passion. These are the times to create the positive change you were born to vision. These are the times for spiritual warriors to come together. These are the times for all spiritual warriors to come together, to listen and collaborate and power in the new template of humanity.

This resource is a powerful emotional and emotive template that can create incredible change. Spiritual warriors are in touch with this resource and a healthy emotional spectrum is a gift in a life and world where every experience and vision is aligned to love humanity and earth.

The heart is big, the vision vast and the power infinite to ignite the critical change for now. No more complaining, the new spiritual warrior tackles the world, fears, and enable solutions when all hope is lost. Sincerely, every spiritual warrior should come forward and seek other spiritual warriors.

This develops incredible accelerated transformation and awareness frontiers, positive change and opening of new ways forward without obstruction.

The new high-frequency templates demolish outdated templates. This is evolution. This is the right way. The new spirituality template lives in the world, loves the world and takes action to create positively and consciously in the world. Here every positive thought and action matters in the world we create for tomorrow. The new spiritual warrior knows and lives passionately to uphold this every day.

As I write this final chapter in 2015, the power of Ancient Egypt has been borrowed in the name of Isis in the name of Islamic State. Isis is an unmistakable icon of peace for world, undoubtedly one of the most recognized earth mother archetypes of all…and yet here it has been cruelly distorted.

This crisis represents the continuous cycles of theft of peace from world and humanity. We are being called to make a stand for peace and love as one. Knowledge has been used to engineer the power of global political-religion elites for centuries.

This is not new. Conventional Egyptology has also denied the essential information we need to know now. This too is not new. If the missing information is the *COSMIC TEMPLATE*, this is the critical gateway to new humanity and world change. *This new world age can open the door to action that is positive and good. The template is ignited as more individuals awaken and join this incredible movement of mission for humanity and earth.*

Elite power structures have deliberately chosen destructive stories to obstruct the evolution of humanity but what is now entirely new is the immense scale. It is a turning point of a profound inner search for truth. Let your meditation and transformation practice guide you in journeys of truth.

This is the important switch to 'opt in' and 'opt out'. Your magnificent stories are the stories of tomorrow. You have the opportunity to change your stories and create the future of a new world today.

Let us take a look at population growth estimates from 1760 to 2014. I hope these figures move you to change. The world population estimate is 70 million in 1760. The world population estimate is 2,000,000, 000 in 1927. The world population estimate is 4,370,000,000 in 1979. The world population estimate is 6,000,000,000 in 1999. The world population estimate at 13:25 on 25 September 2014, is a massive 7,263,100,524.

I watch the counter, the world crisis is magnifying. But watch the counter again, magnificent stories are magnifying and with every individual who is positive change, the world begins to sparkle in magical transformation, synchronicities, loving telepathy and time-bending miracles and solutions to shape a better world.

These are the individuals I want to meet, collaborate with and change the world with. The Source Codes ignite in higher and higher frequency, the spirituality of dreams!

It is time for all of us to count in creating magnificent change.

One Thought for World Peace is a simple global initiative and bond that requests individuals to choose a moment in time in their day to consciously contribute to world peace.

> *Close your eyes, create the space and time to journey within.*
> *Allow your breath to travel with your focus inwards. Allow your*
> *breath to travel outwards in peace. Continue this conscious*
> *breath cycle.*
>
> *What is your vision of your magnificence? Focus on this vision.*
>
> *What is your vision of magnificence for world? Focus on this*
> *vision.*
>
> *Love this vision. Hold this vision in the heart of earth and*
> *humanity.*
>
> *It will take one minute of your time for you to make a difference.*
>
> *Five deep breaths. One, two, three, four, five. Anchor down*
> *through your feet and take a breath. And open your eyes.*
>
> — *ONE THOUGHT FOR WORLD PEACE*

BOOK TWO

• • •

Source Codes Meditations

Introduction

I will be sharing my top tips on three decades of meditation practice and experiencing the best of world meditation and spirituality traditions. If you haven't already, please visit my film archives at *www.traceyash.com*. These films show you high frequency and the energy levels possible when you practice meditation. This takes you into groundbreaking and magnificent transformation, awareness and manifestation possibilities.

The films show you some of the meditations from this book helping you create magnificent stories! These films show me unlocking magic, miracles, love and super-speed manifestation that have transformed my journeys to create a deeply enriching and purposeful life of sharing and giving to others.

What can meditation do – not only for you but also for your greatest love, family, friends and community around you? Meditation in the West is often connected with weird associations and not living in the everyday reality.

Often meditation practitioners don't really travel the journey deep enough into knowing and healing self and ultimately the gift of transforming self is often missed. I address these frustrating, duality driven, outdated and limited wallpaper approaches when teaching individuals at every level. This is the way to excellence.

MEDITATION IS NOT A VACATION. If you use meditation for vacation purposes to avoid self and life, then this approach won't tackle and transform your life. It won't transform you, it won't manifest for you, it won't deliver the peace and happiness you desperately wish for.

This approach won't get the critical transformation job done and you will literally be hanging on to a tantalizing but miserable dream of eventual breakthrough, success, peace, happiness, health… whatever your dream may be.

MEDITATION IS ABSOLUTELY ABOUT GETTING THE JOB DONE: RESOLUTION, EMPOWERMENT, PEACE, SUCCESS AND MAGNIFIENCE.

We will be keeping this super-simple.

Often the pitfalls are not identifying the purpose of meditation and maintaining your passion in regular practice. Don't read this book and think you know it all. Read this book and do the exercises again and again. Know them, love them and in exploring, you know Self a little more every time. This is authentic self exploration and transformation.

This is the true path of meditation mastery. This is deeper inner knowledge, awareness and transformation. This is the journey to a healthier *WHOLE SELF* and this work is continuous and based in discovering and being authentic. Authentic meditation practice enhances authentic living. The deeper and more applied your meditation practice, the deeper life becomes and this is magnificent and absolutely priceless.

Go straight to Page 113 *if you feel ready, eager to start the Meditations but there are some points I offer below that can deepen your experience.*

I would like you to first consider this question before you even begin an exercise. *WHY MEDITATION?* It is also useful even if you already have a practice in place to be authentic, of pure intention, and stripped back, to create the heart of your meditation practice again. Passion and sparkle is often lost. I value the child-like wonder that the first steps into meditation bring.

Knowing this helps you to re-spark your passion and ignite powerful practice so you self-inspire and self-motivate to enjoy a delightful and incredible journey with meditation that can change your world. Imagine if the journey of knowing yourself unlocked more and more magic in your life. I believe this is what can be created if you apply yourself.

A limited version of self can always be accessed or a fleeting magnificent self... but the real magnificence –is knowing you can find magnificence within, at any moment. The meditation practice then becomes a life resource for awareness and brilliance and this will transform your life in untold miraculous ways, events and people.

You can create a brilliant, brilliant life if you are willing to enter the brilliant, super-authentic self-work that breaks illusions. *Are you willing to do that work on yourself?* I am passionate about this path of meditation that can potentially unlock you forever... if you apply yourself forever... and that is the *TRUTH!*

TIP

The Questions To Ask Yourself:

- *Why meditate?*
- *Why are you meditating?*
- *What do you want from meditation?*
- *What do you want to enhance or change within Self?*

People often define an infinite number of reasons for exploring meditation, transformation and manifestation. The less generic your answer the better! Your personality, your stories and purpose are unique. Meditation can bring you positively to life! Feel your way into your unique reasons for meditating, transforming and manifesting.

It often helps you to scan your history for the reasons behind why you are reading this book. It is more than a good idea or because a friend recommended it. What is your deeper purpose for knowing and transforming self? Close this book for a moment, connect with the frequency template of this book, this will help you, and ask what your vision of your most magnificent self is.

The next world phase is about knowing self and self responsibility...generic identification has taken us on a path of being controlled by elite super-structures and programming, and knowing your self is the only way to bust these frustrating and outdated systems.

Don't meditate to cope with what the world serves up but to design a self and life that is as magnificent, free, peaceful, happy, loving, purposeful as can be. Strive consciously to exist magnificently in all. This creates the magnificence of positive change.

If my goal is simply coping then I omit the magnificence that can be mine – brilliance, health and creativity that life can sparkle in. Life serves up chances, brilliant chances and opportunities for incredible life experiences. I see every meditation and every moment in life as an opportunity to enter something much, much greater if we give ourselves the chance. The magnificent divine!

Our beliefs lead the way in how we shape and create reality. If we expect brilliance then we will experience and create it in many, many ways no matter what our circumstances.

TIP

Meditation Alchemy

Let go of excuses... *LET GO OF WORRY ABOUT HOW...* go for your dreams (the most spectacular dreams) and create magnificence. I have created a life that I love. It is an adventure with incredible people and life experiences to remember. This life is the power that transforms and empowers me through challenging times.

It is the energy of greater creativity, choice and contribution. In meditation that ignites your dreams, you can travel beyond fears, limitation and random glimpses of wholeness that prevent you from creating a magnificent life. Burning the fear is also about being 100% authentic. Accepting who you are and working from the foundations of your life experiences; this will solidly grow who you are.

Working with thousands of individuals has taught one thing. *Change will always come.* Transformation will eventually come. Good quality meditation can accelerate this process. How? Trauma takes us right out of body, to opt out of living and engaging in enriching, life opportunities. Meditation that works is alive in the moment and will accelerate the usual transformation processes. You will sparkle in awareness and grasp magic and opportunities to deepen the meaning of existence.

Time heals as we know. But what if you knew exactly how to accelerate these processes. The right meditation processes will accelerate the time frameworks of transformation and manifestation so you can spend more of your life unlocked, healthier and brilliantly alive. *THE FIRST KEY IS FOCUS IN THE NOW.*

Be prepared to give yourself the time and space to anchor and experience the meditation process. Really consider how you are going to spend these minutes meditating. Sleeping or awake in the process? Aware of what is surfacing within self to be transformed or surrendered. Aware of your potential and freedom for change within every thought, feeling and breath. Your preparation and focus into now and body-mind is key.

Your body-mind contains the stories of all you have experienced in your life. With this impeccable focus in mind and body you will impact powerfully and positively your transformation and manifestation journeys.

TIP

Practice High Frequency

LOVE, TRANSFORMATION, MANIFESTATION

Here is a really interesting session I did recently. It came at just the right time when I was finalizing this book and absolutely I could not resist including it. The client wanted to understand the Law of Attraction that has saturated the human potential market. Her comment was, '*Why doesn't it work?*

Let me identify why. Often there is missing information that is essential. However, manifestation will only take place if you truly commit to authentic inner-change work.

You are your stories and these will be played out and manifest to be transformed. This is the path of authentic life work that every individual on this planet undertakes, whatever the programming.

Undertake meticulous self-awareness, allow the stories to surface and be committed to changing your stories. For example, if you continuously play out a story of failing, run through these stories and heal them. Play with the stories; vision and manifest new endings.

Meditation can be used to transform possibilities in our life journeys. Results can only be transformed if we change our frequency. Changing frequency brings peace, resolution and the opportunity to create greater and happier endings. Meditation processes can be tailored to optimize the stories of life.

TIP

Practice Awareness

Knowing self, knowing your stories ignites authenticity, responsibility and acceptance of your role in your life experiences. It may be a great idea here to write down the niggling repeater stories! But don't stop there! Here, it is important to focus on self, to draw out the life learning and wisdom you have awakened because you have lived life.

Maintain the belief that spirituality is about living and the life experiences that teach us, transform us, grow us. Essentially knowing your stories is the journey of love for self and for others. It is the journey of knowing and doing without harm. It is fascinating to note here the stories created around what awareness is and what it can be.

Historical stories have squeezed awareness to the sidelines of society when awareness is a powerful detector of truth. If awareness is muffled then the inauthentic stories spun by elite structures can continue to exist. Whether it is family or society. It is interesting to note the third eye is the missing gateway between right and left brain.

This gateway can help us vision our dreams for better self and world. Removing awareness removes us from greater conscious responsibility to create the world we exist in. *In awakening the key that is the third eye we ignite awareness beyond and in time.* We are conscious of history and the choices made that impact future. In awakening the third eye we also access conscious flow into future and know the world has the opportunity to be a better place.

One thing for certain is that change will always create evolution, however stubborn elite power structures are in cementing illusions. Truth and evolution is the key for all eternity despite the times we live in or adopt as reality. Now how incredible is that!

TIP

Practice Transformation

You are aware of your obvious stories and repeater stories… hitting the right frequency in meditation is key. Peace provides the template to change and enhance your stories. Meditation that powers peace, powers in more opportunities to accelerate your transformation journeys, unlocking you more.

This is why the divine feminine is a missing link in so much information for solid progress and evolution. I shall speak out on a limb; transformation process can be super-accelerated if we know how to incorporate and work with both peace and action simultaneously. Here we surrender, transform and shift manifestation potential.

This is the new and next world phase of evolution. *TRANSFORM OLD TO CREATE NEW.* This is why peace is often regarded as the soft option. Yet, peace brings the power and awareness for action and where necessary the polarity that shows the way to warrior-ship and the path of the hero. Knowing peace brings knowing. Every day use awareness to transform your stories, to discover the most magnificent stories.

The most magnificent stories show you the path of love, authenticity and manifestation that is for greater good. If our journeys in life are conflicted, it is a path that ultimately creates unhappiness, limitation and illness at every level. If we tackle inner conflict primarily we can enter a new template of potential, well-being and health. This ultimately impacts the bigger picture template and dreams and possibilities for a new humanity and better world.

This is exactly what new warrior-ship is about. This takes us right out of trite spirituality. This takes us into tackling who we are, what needs to be awakened and transformed within self, so we can live and contribute magnificently. Putting this off, delays your own healing and helping the world we exist in.

Being a healer in every sphere of life is not about propping the self up behind techniques and philosophies that belong to a master teacher. Being a healer, being a player, being a positive influencer is about healing the most important stories within self. These stories can often be painful but when we discover peace, these stories offer ultimate wisdom that ignites unsurpassed magnificence.

Unsurpassed magnificence is humble, authentic peace that is priceless in wisdom and awake in the brilliant journey that is life. Life is the spiritual journey and every encounter is designed for the choice to make freedom part of the new template…if you believe and love in your heart and mind, you will have greater and greater choice that unlocks freedom and absolutely new paths and new templates for positive evolution and change.

Feel and engage with your power to heal old wounds and stories that you never dreamed you could let go. Choose truth, calculate the time you have misspent in repeat stories that deny you love, freedom and incredible manifestation.

Here, we get genuine in our focus and responsibility to change our stories, to create a better self and better world. Popular literature often doesn't get this tough but authentic transformation and manifestation requires meticulous awareness, dedication and responsibility.

Choosing your stories is step one. Choosing to create magnificent stories in life is the ultimate step and this is the new template of humanity. This is the ultimate in consciousness dancing in polarities that grow and unfold who you are. This is the power accelerator to ground breaking you…redefining all possibilities of self and the stories you have created in your life.

This is the WOW! we have been dreaming of in the human potential field. Here, love and awareness exists in peace and action, here space accelerates manifestation and knowing who we are and the purpose of existence. How deep you go with this path of transformation is entirely up to you. With every passing day, layers unpeel to reveal the true meaning of your magnificence and existence.

This is magnificent inner work.

Following, I offer you a Fifteen-day Meditation process.

Source Codes Meditations

DAY ONE Meditation

TEMPLATES OF MANIFESTATION

What do you need to change in your life? We will be working with practical, simple exercises that will unlock you into high frequency.

Ready with pen and journal. List the toxic issues, present in your life, today only. List the positives in life. What positive thinking and structures do you need to bring to your life now? These lists will change everyday. This is positive and good! Be aware of what is toxic in your life. What are you experiencing as toxic? What is also incredibly positive? What can be incredibly positive for you?

> *Close your eyes. Feel the power of what can be incredibly positive for you. And then make the decision for positive awareness and more positive experiences in life. Five cycles of deep breaths. One, two, three, four, five. Anchor down through your body and use gravity. Five cycles of deep breaths. One, two, three, four, five.*
>
> *Open your eyes.*

Meditation doesn't have to be pedestrian. You can experience changing stories and creative transformation processes. When the journey is neutral you resolve more and create more, and modify positively. Call this simply a *MODIFICATION, REDESIGN, UPSCALING*, a matter of absolute necessity to create a magnificent you. This is super-practical, to be done everyday!

You can read the books, take the notes from your greatest gurus and masters but you have to choose to live it. You do this as a matter of no-nonsense, spiritual practicality. See this work as doing the life vision basics. This high-frequency sovereignty inter-weaves the fabric of life. Your inner work is a life essential rather than an added extra in your schedule, meditation or class to surface-smooth away your day or even who you are.

New meditation technology can be at the forefront of your health and well-being excellence because *it creates the peace that manifests miraculous change.* This super-transforms your health and well-being – improving your life and how you choose to live it. Isn't this information incredible? When we choose magnificent transformation we also choose magnificent health.

Our health then mirrors the brilliance of our life force, not the depletion of it! So out go the mop-up healing operations that mirror your conflict with your life vision and authentic purpose. Meditation becomes a vital life vision tool, not a temporary good idea, hobby or fad. It powers and manifests your magnificent purpose and destiny!

You choose to bring yourself to life and magnificence every day. This way you increase change and progress where it matters most – in life, choosing to create freedom daily.

You are not magnificent until you choose to live it!

TIP

Create It!

Many people ask me for help, finding it difficult and impossible to translate spirituality and spiritual ideas into daily life especially in the West! This reinforces an illusion in terms of where spirituality actually fits in our lives.

If we allow it, we don't know how to make it really work successfully for us. This becomes immensely frustrating and takes you right back into low-frequency! Yet, spirituality is a magnificent life force. It is time to drop the non-truths on what spirituality is and what it can achieve!

TIP

Practice High Frequency

With more high-frequency practice, the more magnificent you become. This is a sacred journey of high frequency. Choose not to return to old, low-frequency stories – you have the tools to change your stories and the choice to create a fine spiritual masterpiece.

Create reminders, sticky notes, and dates with beautiful sunsets, spectacular friends and activities to ignite your magnificence. You become stronger in high-frequency magnificence by creating a schedule of magnificence even when life challenges. You embrace the challenging moments with acceptance and flow.

This is the new paradigm of how we understand how we create our stories and finally see ourselves in truth that is powerfully magnificent. The stories of non-truth can fade easily. We accelerate through positive, high frequency. The entry into this world is only truth. You can always delay your healing processes with distractions but the hunger game will go on. Why wait when you can start to miraculously transform in life and create incredible stories?

Areas of life and world that are visibly not working because the inner landscape requires modification, you simply need to move away from. Thinking is re-set. You are constantly aware of a changing inner landscape that may need to be transformed and awakened in new ways. You act upon this.

This new paradigm in human potential is all about faster, high-frequency processes of transformation, awakening, creativity and synchronicities. This brings in new spiritual technologies and meditation technologies that work harder for you more than ever before. These technologies must be bound with our daily lives.

TIP

Life Becomes Meditation

The big revolution is that your life is a meditation. That's when you are living and creating magnificent healing and health. That is when you hit super-resonance, where you are power-healing. You now enter the revolution of upgraded mind and heart: taking you into the high frequencies that ignite telepathy, passionate creativity and resource, positive synchronicities, positivity and miracles more powerful than a world tinged in low-frequency duality.

The old paradigms of low-frequency can dig deep to prevent every individual's right to freedom and evolution. We owe it to every individual and child to change our low-frequency stories so limitations end with us. *In doing so the fabric of communities change and this is the revolution.*

The revolution is high frequency.

DAY TWO Meditation

THE KUNDALINI SWITCH

Each chakra is a gateway to powerful psychological and physical transformation that enhances health, super awareness and well-being excellence, taking you into the critical human potential and manifestation excellence!

The Chakra system relates to the body/mind as follows: Chakra one, root or muladhara; chakra two, sacral or svadhishtana; chakra three, solar plexus or manipura; chakra four, heart or anahata; chakra five, throat or vishuddha; chakra six, third eye or ajna; chakra seven, crown or sahasrara (note the sanskrit link with Egyptian RA).

This chakra system is duplicated above the crown from eight to fourteen. This is the gateway to anchor in the new higher frequency cosmic templates.

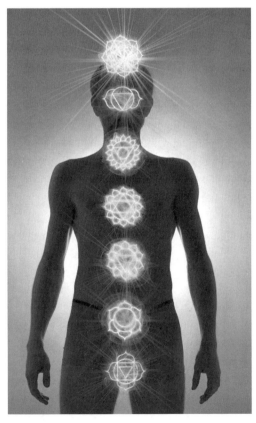

Chakra System: from chakra one to chakra seven.

Caduceus And Kundalini Switch

The Kundalini switch or Caduceus is a process of intensive transformation that rebalances low-frequency trauma encrypted in the physical body and energy field. The cadeuceus remains a symbol of modern medicine today.

Kundalini may be described as awakening of chi, ki, prana, life-force, serpent energy, divine force, light, consciousness or spirit. This is what takes us into health and human potential magnificence.

Whether we meditate regularly or enter meditation for the first time in this book, the starting point is exactly the same – it is you. At every level of practice, you can achieve better meditation results, helping to evolve your practice regularly.

Often we do not clearly assimilate what we want from meditation practice and then our vision and purpose of meditation is not clear. Having clear objectives, whether it is simply defining a magnificent meditation or manifesting health excellence will help you to progress and manifest the life changing benefits.

Remember, your awareness will direct the vision and purpose of your meditation practice to deliver exactly what you need to manifest in your life. At other times you will require energy enhancement, deepest silence and peace, creativity and manifestation, beautiful transformation and surrendering.

Be aware of the importance of knowing what you need to bring to your meditation practice, transformation and manifestation possibilities.

Caduceus.

TIP

Loving Meditation

Please see the following illustration. This can be adapted for meditation sitting on a chair or lying down. Be aware of what suits your body. The alignment here is critical. This helps you to refine both stillness and awareness in meditation practice.

Awareness allows you to listen to your stories and become aware of what you opt in to. You would not require this posture if you are in the workplace. You may love to use this posture if you are home, in nature or at sacred sites. **My tip** is to be alive and aware during the meditations sessions.

In every session, please be mindful and you will accelerate your meditation excellence. Interestingly, you become the sacred temple; wherever you are you adjust your practice to enter meditation excellence. This means creating the time, space and the best self in every meditation. This will impact knowing and manifesting excellence in your life.

By simply falling in to this alignment during your day, you will experience more magnificence, awareness and inner peace that is invaluable in the quality of your daily life.

Adapt your Meditation Practice to Life.

- Define your time, space, peace and posture for meditation and be awake to maximise the meditation experience, transformation and manifestation possibilities.
- Be mindful of body/mind alignment. Practice feeling comfortable with several postures before meditation sessions begin. You need this solid foundation of alignment in place to ground and anchor your experience in the body and world you exist in. This is super-practical meditation. The stories encrypted in your body can be super-transformed, opening the door to manifestation possibilities and change. This is super-speed meditation that delivers transformation and manifestation results if you follow this super-important point! Body/mind alignment can be enhanced by simply following the in-breath at each chakra and holding you internal focus in the power of your body, heart and mind. Spend time exploring this. These are steps that can be often deleted. Re-visit again and again whatever your level of practice.

`TIP`

Loving Breath

Conscious, slower breathing automatically soothes us into peace. As your meditation practice deepens you will use the breath to enter the gateway of transformation and manifestation with super-ease. In this section, I will share how the breath can enhance your meditation and mastery.

The breath cycle is usually viewed in two active phases – inhale and exhale. In the following meditations, the breath cycle will be practiced in four phases with a powerful pause between inhale and exhale. Spend some time exploring this before attempting meditation practice. Inhale/exhale is active. This is where you can use the breath to maximize your focus and self-work.

For example, inhale with powerful inner focus on a particular story. Pause, exhale… allow the story to evolve and repeat this process during your meditation practice. This is an invaluable tip in enhancing transformation and manifestation results and using meditation and powerful breath cycles to super-accelerate.

You can deepen your meditation practice by becoming deeply aware of the breath and during the pause, deepen awareness. This breath practice will assist your magnificence and awareness. Breath and consciousness are powerfully connected. As you master breath and consciousness, you master your life force, time and ultimately life itself. By slowing your breath, you master self and can meticulously awaken to the stories of transformation that will set you free.

TIP

Loving Awareness

Be aware during meditation. Be aware of your stories. Be prepared to surrender to your stories and also master your stories. Be aware of what is relevant and what is not. Silence will develop during practice so you can assess the value of your stories. Be aware of what is playing out in the body-mind.

The Meditation
The Kundalini Switch

- You will have already considered posture, breath and awareness focus for your meditation practice. Now shift all of your awareness into chakra one. Be aware of any stories and frequency issues at this level. Focus conscious breath and awareness into chakra one. Spend one to five minutes here activating the power of chakra one. Be aware of the cycles of your breath. If challenging stories arise use the meditation zone to inspire solutions. There is always another story...a better story. Breathe. Repeat this process in chakra two. Chakra three and so forth to chakra seven. Be aware that each level is connected. Strong foundations will assist you as you reboot life force in every chakra and move into advanced meditation, transformation and manifestation possibilities. This is a vital point to remember for your greatest magnificence and success! When you transform chakra seven you can start the process again and finish at the heart, chakra four, for grounding powerful unity.
- During each meditation at each chakra, your awareness often powerfully and subtly changes. Allowing this is critical for transformation and manifestation excellence. This is the vital fluidity in meditation and necessary in life. Regular practice uses your time effectively to achieve the best transformation and manifestation results. Practice meditation with eyes closed and eyes open. Practice walking meditations and activities meditations with the meditations in this book. This brings meditation and spirituality to the heart of your life!
- Maintain focus into each chakra one to seven; the building blocks of magnificence. Each chakra is worked with meticulously for several minutes equally from one to seven. Repeating this exercise regularly brings outstanding inner knowledge, transformation and manifestation

possibilities that outperform conventional expectations and structures.
- Here you have the solid, simple foundation that can complement other meditation practices, visioning or manifestation goals. You must master your stories to transform and manifest magnificence. The magnificent results come from your authentic, magnificent inner work! Be aware of your body-mind alignment before opening your eyes and engaging with the flow of life once again. You should feel alive, magnificent and grounded in life! Simply, acknowledging this will ignite your life force immediately in your life. This is invaluable for enhancing, empowering and manifesting miracles and magic every day! You are switched on, in highest frequencies possible, at this time for you. *This is the best we can do!* Even better best, is working on high frequency again and again! High frequency overwrites our outdated stories within and ignites the power to overwrite outdated stories within our world. This is the most invaluable, modern world resource for evolution!

TIP

Loving Your Practice

Decide how much time you can comfortably commit to. Be realistic. When is the best time for you to practice meditation? Are your energy levels better morning or night? Time is not usually the issue but your use of it. Do not make time management an excuse for not doing meditation. When you begin to meditate or choose to upscale meditation practice you are committing to life vision change, transformation and manifestation.

If you seek magnificent change, your meditation practice becomes central to life style enhancement and excellence. Let's help you so you can decide clearly how best you should proceed. Check your schedule for the next days and decide where five or ten minutes regular meditation fits easily. If you have an easy schedule you can work more practice into your schedule.

In the beginning, I recommend starting meditation sessions of five to ten minutes. If you have a meditation practice in place, I recommend using the five or ten minute bites to enhance magnificence consciously during your day. Whether beginner or advanced meditator the focus is exactly the same, regular practice will define magnificence and awareness in more and more of your life.

You can be more flexible, if your day is busy, four of five sessions of five minutes may be more satisfactory than the stress of dedicating yourself to thirty minutes practice. Be super-kind to yourself. We live in a modern world. Many meditation practices are ancient in source and do not account for how much technology and how many people are on this planet! Our magnificence is absolutely required in our daily lives so meditation practice needs to firmly connect with this.

I often find myself in blissful meditations in the heart of Cities and airports. This increases a sparkling life force! And others see it and feel it! Your meditation practice improves by using your environment and life experiences to hold and choose magnificence wherever you are. This is super-advantageous when it comes to living authentic magnificence every day in the real world.

This is where your spirituality and magnificence really matters. New meditation is not about being hidden but powerfully alive, awake and at peace in a deep sense of belonging. At one with yourself, and at one with the world.

DAY THREE Meditation

TEMPLATE OF MAGNIFICENT WARRIOR · OSIRIS

This is the next template of understanding our existence and enhancing purpose and human value at every level of life.

Osiris

An icon of immortality and eternity.

This meditation activates Osiris in chakras one and seven to ground unity (1+7=8). This is a fearless template to ignite. Chakra one is key in defining and transforming your stories and frequency of your life vision today. Everyday chakra one will evolve and change. This awareness is key to you building your magnificence. Awareness allows you to transform your stories and manifest new journeys in life. Chakra seven is key to highest frequency Source Codes that take you into the new cosmic template.

- Prepare for meditation as outlined earlier. Focus into chakra one and chakra seven, intensify breath and body-mind awareness. Focus upon OSIRIS. Place this key in chakra one, then chakra two. You will spend a minimum of five minutes in each chakra.
- Be aware of your changing stories and new possibilities every time you meditate. Maintain body-mind awareness, re-set high frequency and maintain super-power in each chakra.
- You can repeat-process in one meditation. This switches you on to the potential of high-frequency templates and practices.

This is a super-simple yet super-effective daily meditation practice. Do not under-estimate critical inner work, simple meditation processes and meticulous awareness to achieve high-frequency excellence. This resets high frequency for more powerful transformation and awareness potential, and stronger energy levels for action and inner peace.

This is the next level of understanding our existence and enhancing purpose and human value at every level of life.

New Templates of Destiny

In meditation practice, individual purpose and destiny is the key in entering the new template of humanity. Using meditation to refine listening to your purpose and destiny will allow incredible spiritual awakening and deepest transformation for this is the truth, the absolute truth of who you are.

Despite stories and 'wall-papering' that muffles this one truth, meditation will reveal more and more about who you are, your purpose, unlocking your destiny in incredible frequencies that indeed do make a difference in the world and communities you experience every day.

Make time to meditate on your purpose. Refine what your purpose may be, moment by moment, in meditation practice and life. Every day you can access a little more, a little deeper understanding. Humility is required as you enter knowing, drop arrogance and you enter what can be an eternal journey of knowing and understanding who you are.

The path of destiny is the only path of truly knowing yourself. Here, you must surrender to the very purpose of your existence and your contracts of learning and wisdom. Surrendering to destiny, concerns absolute honesty and integrity.

I understand within my own destiny, my path is to fully share the way forward into the new higher frequency templates. These templates provide profound archetypes to transform and create a greater self and world. These templates are richer in the meaning of our existence and powerful new energetic structures that demolish and leave behind limiting thoughts/beliefs. My path is to educate not generically but uniquely, each individual to manifest the most magnificent purpose and life.

Despite all illusions you make, when you make them, if you don't awaken, you create for the next generations too. This is what being a new healer is, a positive influencer, breaking with rigid convention to be incredible change. When we listen deep, deep down to the path of destiny, life makes sense, life experiences are resolved, we surrender in peace. We become who we are because we have stopped fighting.

The path of destiny holds the path of silence and the path of new warrior-ship close. This is an intelligent path that defeats the generic, the lacklustre life that too many individuals accept and keep on creating. For two decades I have upheld that healing is about asking the right question.

Bring purpose to the lives and life experiences of individuals and this understanding heals all. No technique. Our lives are spent wandering to find this. This is the key to all great spiritual work. The magical simplicity is about asking the right questions. The simplicity and delight can be missed because we create an arrogance that we know it all or deplete in random over-processing rather than the journey of meditation itself.

In reckoning we know it all we know nothing and life takes this on. To always have purpose, in all that we do creates meaning. Meaning creates a rich fabric of life that is powerfully loving and transformational. It is only this that allows us to hop into the next template.

No matter what we read and how hard we try, this vital initiation requires exact simplicity and purest heart. When we have this in place, we understand why we are here and what we were born, without question, to create and share.

The very nature of our existence and value of it rests in the relationship we have with ourselves. In knowing self, we can love and know others more deeply and help them to be everything and more. This is the new template that will create incredible opportunity and potential for humanity and world in the next millennia.

Peace is absolutely the reality of recognizing purpose and destiny and living it brings the magnificence that so far has only been dreamed. Here is the non-generic and here we have unique individual responsibility that belongs in this time and world. Living spirituality, awake, aware and absolutely loving. It is here, life becomes precious and every individual on the planet can be understood, honoured and loved.

Every individual counts to make a difference. I believe this deeply. It is our individual responsibility to be the change no matter what and create the spark of divinity that is missing. This is the story that now needs to be ignited in one and many.

DAY FOUR Meditation

TEMPLATE OF LOVE · HATHOR

This is the next template of man and woman in magnificent awareness and loving intelligence that creates a better world.

Hathor

Gold of the Gods, 'Hathor the Great, Mistress of Denderah.'

This meditation activates Hathor in chakras two and six (2+6=8). Chakra two contains the stories and frequencies of you as male or female. This is the gateway to more magnificent relationships and creating an enriching world. Chakra six is key to your super-awareness and increasing intelligence. Peace is required for intelligent awareness that knows self and others deeply. Peace allows pure love and healing.

This is critical in a new template of love for self and humanity and enhancing relationships, friendships and value of life. *This meditation activates pineal vision awakening.* Without peace you do not enter extra-sensory abilities and the magic of super-consciousness. Here loving thoughts powerfully manifests and transforms perceived limitations.

- Prepare for meditation as outlined earlier. Chakra two contains the stories and frequency template of you as man or woman. This is key to unlocking magnificent relationships.
- Chakra six is key to a new super-awareness template and increasing intelligence levels. This meditation is for profound pineal vision awakening.
- Focus in chakra two and chakra six, intensify your awareness, body-mind, breath and Hathor.
- Repeat-process in this meditation. This switches you on to repeatedly choosing high frequency.

This is a super-effective practice. Practice focus of chakra six merging perfectly with chakra two. The breath-flow focus also perfectly merges. Maintain this focus to ignite new life force for health, well-being and life excellence.

You create critical inner peace and resolution, essential in the times we live in, to be free of outdated male or female stereotypes and stories. This is the next level of man and woman in magnificent awareness and loving intelligence that creates a better world.

New Templates Of Peace

In meditation practice, this is one of the most important paths to be mastered. Practice redefines how we master silence in intense daily life. In the modern world, we often live white-noise, wall-papered over white noise; effectively the path of silence can unlock us from the distractions of every day living that deplete our magnificence and breakthrough transformation. Knowing silence through meditation is key.

Silence helps us to cut through the layers of wallpapered wounds to access the magnificent self. The magnificent self heals all in a miraculous instant. When I ride out into the Sahara to enter a greater void of silence, I embrace the space and time, the depth of silence that the desert brings. It is this expanse that we should come to know and feel in meditation practice. Space and time are great allies amidst the demands and distractions of modern living.

The path of silence allows listening to self. The path of silence allows us to listen and love our way to self and others – to trust the journey of love. The path of silence knows what to do and the relevant path of action.

Here timing is impeccable, you feel your way into the silence to intuit the key moments of awareness and the key moments when action is life changing. In a modern world of doing, talking and action, silence is a majestic friend that stands still in space and time to bring you the space and peace you need in your daily, busy modern life that is subscribed to layers of stories that limit who you are and who you can be.

The silence becomes the divine feminine. Beautiful, spacious, conscious silence that can be engaged with to enhance quality of life and the quality you present to the world you exist in. The silence drives your awareness to hold fine quality at the heart of every action, pause, thought and word.

DAY FIVE Meditation

TEMPLATE OF HERO · HORUS

This is the next template of transformation and manifestation where old stories of pain, suffering and conflict are no longer handed down to future generations.

Horus

HER OR HORUS is symbolized in the icon of the hawk with raised wings. This is also a powerful source of Ancient Egyptian Pharaonic rule. HER evolves to the later HORUS and can be translated as *SHINING. HORUS IS THE IMPORTANT SYMBOL OF LIGHT AND SHINING BRILLIANCE. THIS CREATES A LIVING LINEAGE TO THE SHINING ONES WITHIN US. YOUR LIGHT AND BRILLIANCE.* This links you with the oldest of archaic cults.

This meditation activates HORUS in chakra three and chakra five (3+5=8). Chakra three contains the stories and frequencies of your emotional journeys. This is the gateway to the hero, freedom and peaceful happiness. Chakra five is key to magnificent communication and manifestation. This is a ground-breaking template that will transform how you use the emotional spectrum, create time and space for value upon life.

Enhanced health, happiness and new energy levels for magnificent manifestation and communication are created. This brings ground-breaking emotional intelligence and physical healing, igniting new frontiers of awareness and manifestation in your life. This is the next level of transformation and manifestation where old stories of pain, suffering and conflict are no longer handed down.

- Meditation in chakra three and chakra five, your breath-flow and body-mind, HORUS. Be aware of the changing frequencies and new possibilities.
- Meticulous high-frequency awareness in chakra three and chakra five. High-frequency transformation-mediations will remodel any limited stories to enter the gateway of transformation and manifestation magnificence.
- Repeat-process again and again in one meditation. This switches you on in high frequency. Finish in the heart chakra (from chakra one, two, three, four).

DAY SIX Meditation

TEMPLATE OF MAGIC · ISIS

This is the next template of love, forgiveness and compassion – changing the stories of humanity to end war, pain and suffering.

Isis

'I am all that has been, that is, and that will be.' Isis is the personification of faithful wife and devoted mother. Isis is the Mistress Of The Words of Power and the Goddess Of Nature. She is the absolute embodiment of nature and magic.

- Meditate upon ISIS and chakra four (4+4=8). Chakra four is the gateway to heart and humanity magnificence. This is the gateway from our human hearts to divine love. Chakra four is the gateway to the cosmic heart beat; the magnificent gateway.
- You vision and unlock new stories of your heart. Meditate for a minimum of five minutes.

It is essential to repeat-process for effective daily transformation results. Effective high-frequency heart maintains strong and empowered energy field for health excellence that demonstrates *you can* change your frequency and your stories. This is the next level of love, forgiveness and compassion – changing the stories of humanity to end war, pain and suffering.

DAY SEVEN Meditation

HIGHEST FREQUENCIES TEMPLATE

OSIRIS · ISIS · HATHOR · HORUS

Next template of high frequency: visionary, peaceful and empowered for excellence to manifest magnificently.

Meditate upon OSIRIS and chakra one and chakra seven (1+7= 8). This creates a new gateway for transformation and manifestation possibilities.

Osiris

An icon of immortality and eternity in the inner shrine of MAAT.

- Chakra one is gateway to the stories and frequency of your life vision. Chakra seven is gateway to The Source Codes.
- Meditate with meticulous precision upon Osiris and awareness into chakra one and chakra seven.

Meditate upon HATHOR and chakra two and chakra six (2+6= 8) creates new gateway of transformation and manifestation.

Hathor

Gold of the Gods, 'Hathor the Great, Mistress of Denderah',

- Chakra two is gateway to stories and frequency of you as male or female.
- Chakra six: key to super-awareness and intelligence.

Meditate upon HORUS and chakras three and five (3+5= 8) creates new gateway of transformation and manifestation.

Horus

HER OR HORUS is symbolized in the icon of the hawk with raised wings. This is also a powerful source of Ancient Egyptian Pharaonic rule. HER evolves to the later HORUS and can be translated as *SHINING. HORUS IS THE IMPORTANT SYMBOL OF LIGHT AND SHINING BRILLIANCE. THIS CREATES A LIVING LINEAGE TO THE SHINING ONES WITHIN US. YOUR LIGHT AND BRILLIANCE.* This links you with the oldest of archaic cults.

- Chakra three is gateway to the stories and frequencies of your emotional story. The new gateway to hero/heroine and happiness.
- Chakra five: key to magnificent communication and manifestation.

Meditate upon ISIS and chakra four and four DIVINE HEART (4+4=8) creates new gateway to transformation and manifestation.

Isis

'I am all that has been, that is, and that will be.' Isis is the personification of faithful wife and devoted mother. Isis is the Mistress of the Words of Power and the Goddess Of Nature. She is the absolute embodiment of nature and magic.

- Chakra four is gateway to heart and humanity magnificence.
- Chakra four is gateway to the cosmic heart beat – the magnificent gateway.
- Meditate for a minimum ten minutes. Finish meditation grounding through the heart chakra through chakra one, two, three.

This is an intense super-transformation, super-awareness and super-manifestation process that increases with regular practice. You master and activate The Source Codes in life for miracles of transformation and manifestation.

It is essential to repeat-process for effective transformation and manifestation results.

Effective high frequency maintains strong and empowered self for excellence that demonstrates *you can* change your frequency and manifest your dreams magnificently.

Please use a life vision journal daily, exploring the potential of the keys in meditation and in your life vision. Meditate and write down your journeys and visions of transformation and life purpose.

DAY EIGHT Meditation

SPIRITUAL WARRIOR TEMPLATE · RA

Ra

Father of Maat, Re was the source of right and justice in the cosmos.

- Breathe and close eyes to enter your inner world. Inner world can change in any miraculous moment of practice. Be aware to enter these magical moments where all change is possible! Place meticulous awareness into each chakra, one to seven.
- Your awareness remains sharp throughout your practice. The breath detoxifies and magnifies your energy levels and awareness abilities. Alive in mind-body your awareness shapes your transformation and changes your stories. Be aware of each chakra. Be aware of the subtle stories and changes. This will allow you to locate and unlock high frequency. Switch easily between low frequency and shift into high. Your awareness is the change-switch. Spend time in these processes and practice daily. Your awareness becomes fluid.
- Powerful meditation and transformation processes come with gravity, grounding and physicality. Alive and powerful in the body-mind, you will experience life force building. Build life force into awareness of mind-body. The powerful cycles of breath will magnify life force levels. It is here you can change frequency. Be aware of exact life force levels. Be aware of high frequency. Experience, explore and understand what high frequency is. Process how life force feels and is.
- Meticulous awareness from chakra one to chakra seven.
- Meditate upon RA into each chakra one to seven. Meditate for two minutes minimum in each chakra.
- Be aware of the stories within each chakra and the possible stories available to you. Choose the most magnificent story at each chakra.
- Meditate upon RA and into each chakra eight to fourteen, located directly above chakra seven; this ignites a new higher frequency template of the Spiritual Warrior.
- Define Spiritual Warrior and Vision this in your life vision. Here you hold the power to manifest. Finish the meditation in the heart chakra, grounding transformation and high frequency through chakra one, two, three.

DAY NINE Meditation

POWER HEALER TEMPLATE · SEKHMET

Sekhmet

Sekhmet originates from the word 'sekhem' or 'power'. Sekhmet is 'the (one who is) powerful'.

- Meditate upon SEKHMET into each chakra one to seven.
  Meditate for two minutes minimum in each chakra.
- Be aware of the powerful stories within each chakra and the possible stories available to you. Choose the most magnificent story at each chakra.
- Meditate upon SEKHMET and into each chakra eight to fourteen, located directly above chakra seven; this ignites a new higher frequency template of the Healer Warrior.
- Define Healer Warrior and vision this in your life vision. Here you hold the power to manifest. Finish the meditation in the heart chakra, grounding transformation and high frequency through chakras one, two, three.

DAY TEN Meditation

TIME TRAVELLER TEMPLATE

SHU · TEFNUT

Shu

As air, Shu was considered to be cooling and a pacifier. Due to the association with air, calm, to *Ma'at* (truth, justice and order).

Tefnut

The product of parthenogenesis, and involves some variety of bodily fluid.

- Now for Source Codes reboot. Meditate upon SHU-TEFNUT into chakras one, two, three, and so on, to each chakra. Use the breath powerfully and consciously to connect each level.
- Be aware of your stories but be aware you can change stories easily in The Source Codes. *Create outstanding transformation at each level.* You are aware of outstanding transformation as the exercise intensifies your life force for magnificent change.
- Every meditation that is completed with exact precision and passion unlocks greater life force. Here is some critical information. You are transforming to anchor The Source Codes. *You are transforming to increase new levels of life force resource that unlock you from low-frequency stories and coping strategies of limiting meditation and transformation technologies.*
- *Source Codes and high-frequency life force is locked into your health, well-being and daily life.* This time is critical to be able to access the technologies that work, deliver breakthrough and freedom from the toxic cycles of low-frequency stories. This is the modern Spiritual Warrior who creates a reality of excellence, time and energy resource.
- Be conscious of travelling into magnificent possibilities to transform and awaken you.
- Meditate upon Shu-Tefnut and chakra eight to chakra fourteen located directly above chakra seven. This is the new cosmic template. You can ignite the new higher frequency template of the Time Traveller. Travel in time to past and future stories, transform and enhance these stories.
- You become increasingly powerful in manifesting super-transformation during your daily meditation practice.

- Finally, ground this meditation into the heart through chakras one, two, three in to four.

The Sphinx, Giza, 2014.

DAY ELEVEN Meditation

TEMPLATE OF WISDOM WARRIOR · THOTH

Thoth

Inventor of writing, the creator of languages, the scribe, interpreter, and adviser of the gods, and the representative of the sun god, Re. Wise counsellor and persuader, and is associated with learning and measurement. Identified by the Greeks with their closest matching god Hermes, with whom Thoth was eventually combined as Hermes Trismegistus.

- Meditate upon THOTH into each chakra one to seven. Meditate for two minutes minimum in each chakra.
- Be aware of the powerful stories within each chakra and the possible stories available to you. Choose the most magnificent story at each chakra.
- Meditate upon THOTH and into each chakra eight to fourteen, located directly above chakra seven; this ignites a new higher frequency template of the Healer Warrior.
- Define Wisdom Warrior and vision this in your life vision. Here you hold the power to manifest. Finish the meditation in the heart chakra, grounding transformation and high frequency through chakras one, two, three.

DAY TWELVE Meditation

PEACE WARRIOR TEMPLATE · ATEN

Aten

The Aten as 'the Prince of Truth' became a source of inner guidance and personal responsibility.

- Meditate upon ATEN and in each chakra and consciousness level. Now for Source Codes reboot. Exact focus.
- *In The Source Codes subtle thought manifestation technologies shape your transformation.* Be aware of your stories but be aware you can change stories easily in The Source Codes. *Precision manifest outstanding transformation at each level.* You are aware of outstanding transformation as the exercise intensifies your life force for magnificent change.
- *Source Codes and high-frequency life force is locked into your health, well-being and daily life.* This Source Codes process will **increase peace, health and spirituality excellence.** This time is critical to be able to access the technologies that work, deliver breakthrough and freedom from the cycles of low-frequency stories.
- Focus ATEN into chakras eight to fourteen located directly above chakra seven, ignites the new template of the Warrior of Peace. This will power you in increased peace resource every day.
- Meditate upon ATEN into each chakra one to chakra seven. Meditate for two minutes minimum in each chakra.
- Be aware of the powerful stories within each chakra and the possible stories available to you. Choose the most magnificent story at each chakra.

DAY THIRTEEN Meditation

TRUTH WARRIOR TEMPLATE · MAAT

Maat

MAAT is synonymous with truth, justice and cosmic order. Here in the Land of Dreams is the gateway to divine feminine wisdom. This MAAT PRINCIPLE governs the ladder or journey of a greater humanity and world.

- Meditate upon MAAT and into each chakra and consciousness level. Now for Source Codes reboot. Exact focus on MAAT into chakras one to seven. Exact focus MAAT in chakras seven to one.
- *Deepen the breath into each chakra with precision focus.* Your awareness is sharp. The breath detoxifies and magnifies your energy resource and awareness abilities. Alive in mind-body your awareness shapes your transformation and changes your stories. *In each chakra and consciousness level, be aware of the subtle changes.* This will allow you to locate and unlock higher and higher frequency. *Be aware of this process continuously in your deepening meditation practice.*
- Focus MAAT into chakras eight to fourteen located directly above chakra seven. Enter the new high-frequency template of the Spiritual Warrior of Truth in this meditation and in life vision.
- Finish this meditation by grounding high frequency into the heart chakra through chakras one, two, three.

The Power of Truth

High frequency gives us entry into awareness so we can untangle ourselves from compromising our magnificence and our healing journeys, and believing stories that impact our magnificence! Compromising your magnificence is about the choices you make, the stories you buy into and the stories you create.

Make another choice and be magnificent in more and more of your life. Living magnificently is about who you are, what you know you are beyond the deep layers of untruths and stories that suffocate your magnificence.

Frequently recognize your magnificence and give yourself the freedom to live it. We can manifest magnificence if we choose. I want you to live in high frequency. I want you to be free. I want you to maintain this.

DAY FOURTEEN Meditation

CREATIVE MEDITATION

Morning

Experiment with sending yourself mobile alerts or sticky notes reminding yourself to remain aware, in the high-frequency zone, in transformation and positivity.

Afternoon

Do nothing. See which one changes the course of your day. This teaches you self-responsibility so when you meditate or attend a seminar you can achieve greater, so much more significant self-work and raise the bar of excellence in your life vision.

We can proceed to move out of self-work that is a more limited mop-up operation and proceed to move quickly through and out of duality. It's an energy hunger game. It's a life force hunger game! So many of us are absolutely starved energetically so it is impossible to change the stories we are aware of! And we let the hunger game go on because we don't know what to do about it!

As a teacher, I love the challenge of undoing low-frequency transformation approaches and expectations that slow these magically important areas of life and breakthroughs you dream of. Spirituality can be magnificent! If we do not generate a magnificent facilitator for ourselves progress can be slow.

What if our meditation is for only relaxation at best? What if decades of meditation do not deliver the breakthroughs you dream but you also deserve? Not that these approaches are totally wrong, just often ludicrously slow and that is the untruth; add in a facilitator who is not awake and your potential transformation is disastrous! That facilitator can't see who you are and who you can be!

And so low-frequency limited-stories continue, absorbing and creating further limitations! And we don't have time (I feel) to bury a magnificent life force and not truly live life. I love energy but without experiencing excellence, transformation processes can be slow and difficult leaving miracles out of reach and out of reality! Locate your magnificence and power-meditate and maintain it! This takes work!

DAY FIFTEEN Meditation

STAR TRAVELLER TEMPLATE · SIRIUS

The Great Pyramid of Giza

The Great Pyramids of Egypt were purposefully designed to express and amplify the power of universe and divinity within every individual and world. Turning elite power off!

- Meditate upon SIRIUS and each chakra and consciousness level, from one to seven. Now for Source Codes reboot.
- *Deepen your breath and awareness into each chakra with precision focus.* The breath detoxifies and magnifies your energy resource and awareness. *Be aware of this process continuously in your deepening meditation practice.*
- *In The Source Codes subtle thought manifestation technologies shape your transformation.* Be aware of your stories but be aware you can change stories easily in The Source Codes. *Precision manifest outstanding transformation at each level.* You are aware of outstanding transformation as the exercise intensifies your life force for magnificent change.
- Every exercise that is completed with exact precision and passion unlocks life force. Here is some critical information. You are transforming to anchor The Source Codes. You are transforming to increase new levels of life force resource that unlock you from low-frequency stories and coping strategies of limiting meditation and transformation technologies.
- *Source Codes and high-frequency life force is locked into your health, well-being and daily life.* This Source Codes process will *increase health and spirituality excellence.* This time is critical to be able to access the technologies that work, deliver breakthrough and freedom from the cycles of low-frequency stories. *This is the modern change-influencer who creates excellence, time and energy resource.*

> *High frequency shifts CONSCIOUSNESS into the Zero Point Field and all possibilities.*

The Great Pyramid of Giza.

- The ancients left considerable clues in architecture and timeless wisdom in their incredible monuments. *Be fully aware of body-mind*, and the wisdom in your body-mind. *No dimension is limited in the Zero Point Field and can be redesigned. The Zero Point Field is what mystics and visionaries enter to access prophecy and miracles of healing. They have been trained and know how to manipulate positively the ZPF. When the ZPF is anchored in this dimension super-speed change appears miraculously.*
- Focus on SIRIUS in chakras eight to fourteen, located directly above seven, ignites the new high-frequency template of The Star Traveller. Finish this meditation by grounding high frequency in the heart chakra through chakras one, two, three.

MEDITATE EVERY DAY to help you manifest positive journeys forward whilst embracing all your stories. You now have the sovereignty and greater freedom to do so.

The best we can do is to maintain the path of the peaceful warrior. When we know this we know when it is necessary to fight. Be aware of the change that can take place within (small beautiful changes) and dream positive change into the world and the collective stories of humanity. *This is the new way.* The positive switch for change and when we work together in communities we can impact magnificent change without unnecessary conflict or expending the resource that impedes critical progress.

Allow yourself to be gifted more and more transformation. Your immense generosity is key and this is only manifest through solid foundations of high frequency. Think about the next level whilst fully accepting who you are today. *Celestial Healing* is not "I am meditating", then stop.

This meditation practice is living, fluid, intelligent, awake and high-frequency effective and will manifest positive change because the technology is intelligent. The meditation technology delivers the very real solutions in the world you exist.

Celestial Healing is *I am practicing meditation and I am learning what meditation can do to create infinite positive change.* It can be anything and everything as long as you do not close down its infinite potential with rigid limiting or dull, generic practice.

Meditation is for discovering and awakening your divine intelligence, freedom and peace to accelerate a new level and story of humanity. The ancients knew this. The story has always been present and is often hidden or deleted.

This is the story of the new template for warriors of positive change. To be passive and inactive is incorrect; you must be both peaceful and active. This is the constant changing entity of meditation, life and humanity. We often do not have the awareness and vocabulary to know this or describe this. It is an abstract, infinite intelligence resource that often evades description.

Knowing it once is not enough. Reading books to know it is also not enough. When we understand and conceptualize this, it is part of our infinite truth and our infinite intelligence. *To deny this we deny our cosmic template and remain insignificant slaves of elite power structures.* We may rally against conspiracy theories but we fail to bust the structures that enslave us.

Meditation is an essential practice and discipline that allows you access to a greater story of humanity. *You become a switch and a key in changing the stories of tomorrow for many more individuals than yourself – if you believe and experience the cosmic template within.*

This is the seed of hope for a greater humanity and loving earth.

Glossary

AKHU

The archetypal cosmic man is central to Ancient Egypt and is found in Hermetic and Gnostic teachings. Akhu is central to the next world phase and evolution of humanity.

ATEN

The Aten as 'the Prince of Truth' became a source of inner guidance and personal responsibility. (Here is a ground-breaking cosmic template for man and earlier roots for later Christianity.) At Akhetaten (Tel-el-Amarna), the axis of Akhenaton's tomb and a small temple of Aten both point to the sunrise of the Spring Equinox, again linking with the resurrection of Osiris.

Akhenaton's programme for the 'Great Aten Temple' was directed upon the 'House of Aten', known as 'The Mansion of the Benben'. The original Benben stone stood in the temple of sun-god Ra (Ra-Horakhty or 'Ra-Horus of the Horizon') at Heliopolis.

DENDERAH ZODIAC

The zodiac is a planisphere of the stars on a plane projection, showing the 12 constellations of the zodiacal band forming 36 decans of ten days each, and the planets. These decans are groups of first-magnitude stars. These were used in the ancient Egyptian calendar, which was based on lunar cycles of around 30 days and on the heliacal rising of the star Sothis (Sirius).

The Denderah Zodiac depicts Twelve zodiacs and the planets: Mercury, Venus, Mars, Jupiter, Saturn, the Moon, Sirius, Orion; the three known constellations of the north: Draco, Ursa Minor and Ursa Major, and the axis of the temple.

GEB

The Great Ennead of Heliopolis comprises of Atum, Shu, Tefnut, Nut, Geb, Osiris, Isis, Seth and Nephtys. Linked with earth, Geb is depicted as the physical support of the world. Geb constituted, with Nut, his sister, the second generation in the Ennead of Heliopolis. In Egyptian art Geb, as a portrayal of the earth, was often depicted lying by the feet of Shu, the air god, with Nut.

HATHOR

Known as 'Female Hawk', 'Cow of Gold', 'Lady of The Sycamore Tree', 'Great Lady of Punt' (Patroness of incense, gold and myrrh), a venomous cobra breathing fire against the king's enemies. Hathor was also known when Ra opened his eyes inside the lotus as it emerged from the primordial chaos and his eyes began to weep, and droplets fell to the ground. They were transformed into a beautiful woman who was named Gold of the Gods, 'Hathor the Great, Mistress of Denderah'.

HELIOPOLIS MYTH

This knowledge and legacy was passed down by the gods through the Creation Myth of Heliopolis and what the Ancient Egyptians regarded as the First Time, 'Zep Tepi', an ancient, ancient time when the neturu lived on earth.

The neteru is the living legacy of The Shining Ones. As 'the Complete One' and 'The Not yet Existent One', Atum rises from the water upon the primordial mound to create the first cosmic pair, neteru, Shu and Tefnut. A realm of radiant light is created. Khepri 'he who becomes' appears in the east horizon. The cosmos begins to unfold, the sky goddess, Nut and earth god, Geb are born to Shu and Tefnut. The separation of Geb and Nut is complete so that Osiris, Isis, Seth and Nephtys can be born from the celestial womb.

> 'O you Great Ennead which is on Ōn(Heliopolis), Atum, Shu, Tefēnet, Gēb, Nūt, Osiris, Isis, Seth, and Nephthys; O you children of Atum, extend his goodwill to his child in your name of Nine Bows.'
>
> — THE PYRAMID TEXTS, 1665 PT

HORUS

HER OR HORUS is symbolized in the icon of the hawk with raised wings. This is also a powerful source of Ancient Egyptian Pharaonic rule. HER evolves to the later HORUS and can be translated as *SHINING. HORUS IS THE IMPORTANT SYMBOL OF LIGHT AND SHINING BRILLIANCE. THIS CREATES A LIVING LINEAGE TO THE SHINING ONES WITHIN US. YOUR LIGHT AND BRILLIANCE.* This links you with the oldest of archaic cults.

ISIS

'I am all that has been, that is, and that will be.' (From The Temple of Isis, at Sais, Ancient Egypt.) Wife and consort Isis, she maintained control but Seth plotted against Osiris and formed a group of conspirators. Seth had the cooperation of a Queen from Ethiopia called Aso (the personification of the burning winds of the South). Seth secretly measured Osiris' body and made a chest corresponding to size. During festivities, the chest was presented and promised to the man who exactly fitted it. Of course, no one but Osiris fitted the chest. The lid was slammed shut, Osiris was trapped and the chest was sent far away to sea.

Osiris was twenty-eight years old (note here the link with the 28 day lunar cycle). Isis wandered everywhere to discover the fate of Osiris. As she reached the Taniatic Mouth, she discovered the chest had been cast down at Byblos.

Isis travelled to Byblos. Here, she transformed into a swallow that hovered around the pillar where the chest was concealed. The King and Queen granted that the chest should be removed. Isis removed the chest to the desert nearby but Seth discovered it, opened it and cut the body of Osiris into 14 pieces, scattering the parts throughout Egypt.

Isis is the personification of faithful wife and devoted mother and the Mistress Of The Words of Power and the Goddess Of Nature. She is the absolute embodiment of nature and magic.

KUNDALINI

A natural process of tangible life force awakened through each energy centre or chakra. Each is a gateway that activates powerful psychological and physical transformation that increases health and well-being.

A range of experiences will occur at these levels should the kundalini process be authentically activated. It is a process of intensive transformational processes that rebalances low-frequency trauma encrypted in the physical body and energy field through each energy centre.

Kundalini may be described as chi, ki, prana, life force, serpent energy, divine force, light, consciousness or spirit. It can be activated spontaneously or with yoga, meditation, psychedelic drugs, plant medicine, subtle energy healing, spiritual awakening, detox programmes, 'out of body experiences', 'near death experiences' and pineal neuropsychology research. *Today Regular meditation practice can increase health excellence.*

MEDITAIION

Almost all cultures worldwide have a form or practice to develop awareness of the moment in prayer, ceremony, ritual, mantra, yoga, tai chi, chi gong, martial arts and meditation. Intentional awareness transforms lives and alleviates suffering, improves capacity to control or regulate emotions, transform emotional dysfunction, evolve and refine emotional programming, decrease negative vision and perspective, reduce depression; changing the imbalance of circuits in the brain.

Advanced, regular meditation and transformation practitioners evolve greater awareness. This creates a journey of self-care, self-love and world awareness that increasingly develops. However, investigations reveal that only regular practice creates outstanding results.

MAAT

MAAT is synonymous with truth, justice and cosmic order. Here in the Land of Dreams is the gateway to divine feminine wisdom. This MAAT PRINCIPLE governs the ladder or journey of a greater humanity and world.

NEITH

Neith's symbol, and part of her hieroglyph resembled a loom, and in later syncretisation of Egyptian myth by the Greeks, Neith was linked with weaving. At this time her role as a creator merged with Athena, as deity who wove all of the world and existence.

NEPHTYS

The Great Ennead of Heliopolis comprises of Atum, Shu, Tefnut, Nut, Geb, Osiris, Isis, Seth and Nephtys. Nephthys was considered the unique protectress of the Sacred Phoenix, or the Bennu Bird. This role may have stemmed from an early association in Heliopolis, which was renowned for its 'House of the Bennu' temple.

NUT

The Great Ennead of Heliopolis comprises of Atum, Shu, Tefnut, Nut, Geb, Osiris, Isis, Seth and Nephtys. A goddess of the *sky* and heavens often depicted as a woman, arched over *Geb*.

OSIRIS

An icon of immortality and eternity in the inner shrine of MAAT. The Great Ennead of Heliopolis comprises of Atum, Shu, Tefnut, Nut, Geb, Osiris, Isis, Seth and Nephtys. Osiris connects us during this period with the similar Celtic Green Man, Roman Attis, Babylonian Tammuz and Sumerian Damuzi.

Osiris is celebrated with the Spring Equinox and resurrection connecting the Great Pyramid site with Christ Consciousness. The cult of Osiris of regeneration and rebirth had a strong association with eternity and immortality. Plutarch recounts one version of the myth in which Seth, with the Queen of Ethiopia, conspired with 72 accomplices to plot the assassination of Osiris.

PINEAL GLAND

The pineal gland, known as the pineal body, conarium or epiphysis cerebri, is a small endocrine gland in our brain. The pineal produces melatonin, a serotonin-derived hormone that affects the modulation of sleep patterns in both seasonal and circadian rhythms. The shape resembles a tiny pine cone that is also a universal symbol of antiquity. It is located in the epithalamus near the centre of the brain, between the two hemispheres.

PRECESSION OF EQUINOXES

The Precession of the Equinoxes is a cycle of 25920 years. The vernal point travels through the twelve constellations. Each twelve months is 2160 years and 3 decans of 720 years. We have also seen these measurements repeated in The Great Pyramid – also known as the 'House of God'.

RA

Many syncretisms were formed between Re and other gods, producing such names as Re-Harakhty and Amon-Re. Aspects of other gods influenced Re himself; his falcon-headed appearance as Re-Harakhty originated through association with *Horus*. The influence of Re was spread from On (*Heliopolis*), which was the centre of his worship. From the Fourth Dynasty, kings held the title 'Son of Re', and 'Re', later part of the throne name at accession. Father of *Maat*, Re was the source of right and justice in the cosmos.

SEKHMET

Sekhmet originates from the word 'sekhem' or 'power'. Sekhmet is 'the (one who is) powerful'. Linked with war and destroyer of enemies of Re. Sekhmet was associated with disease, healing and medicine. Like other fierce goddesses in the Egyptian pantheon, she was called the 'Eye of Re'. She was companion of the god *Ptah* and was worshipped at Memphis. She was depicted as a lioness or as a woman with the head of a lioness, with solar disk and the uraeus serpent.

SETH

Seth was lord of the desert, master of storms, disorder, and warfare. Seth embodied the necessary and creative element of violence and disorder within the ordered world.

SHU

As air, Shu was considered to be cooling and a pacifier. Due to the association with air, calm, to *MA'AT* (truth, justice and order), Shu was portrayed in art as wearing an ostrich feather. Shu was seen with one to four feathers. The ostrich feather was symbolic of *light* and *emptiness*. Positioned between the *sky* and *earth*, he was also known as the *wind*. The Great Ennead of Heliopolis comprises of Atum, Shu, Tefnut, Nut, Geb, Osiris, Isis, Seth and Nephtys.

SIRIUS

the ancient Egyptians understood the Sirius Star System connected with Isis, Hathor and Horus. We also know that according to Mark Lehner, Director of the Giza Plateau Mapping Project, the height of The Great Pyramid is 481 feet or 146.59 metres; this gives 1460 or 1461 years correlating with the Sothic calendar (or Sirius Star system).

Sirius is the brightest star in the night sky. With a visual apparent magnitude of −1.46, it is almost twice as bright as Canopus, the next brightest star. The name 'Sirius' is derived from the Ancient Greek: Seirios ('glowing' or 'scorcher'). The star has the Bayer designation Alpha Canis Majoris.

What the naked eye perceives as a single star is actually a binary star system, consisting of a white main-sequence star of spectral type A1V, termed Sirius A, and a faint white dwarf companion of spectral type DA2, called Sirius B.

SOURCE CODES

Super-Consciousness Resource For Highest Frequency Living.

TEFNUT

Tefnut is a daughter of the solar god Ra-Atum. Consort to her brother, Shu, she is mother of Nut, the sky and Geb, the earth. Tefnut's grandchildren were Osiris, Isis, Set, Nephthys, and in other versions, Horus the Elder (Heru Wer). She was also a great grandmother of Horus the Younger, a member of the Ennead of Heliopolis. There are a number of variants to the myth of the creation of Tefnut and her twin brother Shu. In all versions, Tefnut is the product of parthenogenesis, and all involve some variety of bodily fluid. The Great Ennead of Heliopolis comprises of Atum, Shu, Tefnut, Nut, Geb, Osiris, Isis, Seth and Nephtys.

THE SHINING ONES

This Ennead of Nine comprises of The Most High, the Lord of The Spirits and Seven Archangels. This nine-fold pantheon of God links with The Great Ennead of Heliopolis, Egypt, which was known as On. The Shining Ones were a group of culturally and technically super-advanced people who settled and established an agricultural and teaching epicentre estimated9300–8200 BC.

THE PRIESTS OF HELIOPOLIS

The Priests of Heliopolis were also super-proficient in prophecy, astronomy, mathematics, architecture and magic arts just like The Shining Ones. The Benben stone is also linked to eternity and the Philosopher's Stone.

THOTH

Inventor of writing; the creator of languages; the scribe; interpreter and adviser of the gods, and the representative of the sun god, Re. Wise counsellor and persuader, and is associated with learning and measurement. Identified by the Greeks with their closest matching god Hermes, with whom Thoth was eventually combined as Hermes Trismegistus; also leading to the Greeks' naming Thoth's cult centre as Hermopolis, meaning city of Hermes.

References

Author and publisher gratefully acknowledge all permissions received for quotations used in this book.

p. 21: **Budge, E. A. Wallis**. *The Egyptian Book of The Dead*. Penguin Group. Penguin Classics, 2008.

p. 27: *Edgar Cayce Readings*, # 1486-1, 27-31, copyright © November 26, 1937. www. edgarcayce.org. Edgar Cayce's A.R.E. Association for Research and Enlightenment, 215 67th Street, Virginia Beach, VA 23451. All rights reserved.

p. 36/37: **Broadhurst, Paul & Miller, Hamish**. *The Sun and The Serpent*. Mythos Press, Copyright © 1989. All rights reserved.

p. 38: **Fergusson, James**. *A History of Architecture in All Countries*. 1893.

p. 49: **O'Brien, Christian and Barbara Joy**. *The Genius of the Few* and the Golden Age Project run on behalf of the authors by Edmund Marriage – *www.goldenageproject.org.uk*

p. 50: **Weigall, Arthur**. *The Life and Times of Akhnaton Pharaoh of Egypt*. William Blackwood and Sons. 1910.

p. 64: "Psychological Clearing prelude to Soul Emergence", by Dr Dawson Church. Copyright © 2007 Dr Dawson Church. All rights reserved.

p. 71: "The Rainbow Body" by Gail Bernice Holland, first appeared in the *Noetic Sciences Review*, (March-May 2003, issue number 59, pages 32 and 33), published by the Institute of Noetic Sciences (IONS), quoted with permission of IONS (*www.noetic.org*). All rights reserved. Copyright 2002.

p. 72/73: **Paul Pévet**, *The internal time-giver role of melatonin. A key for our health. www.ncbi.nlm.nih.gov/pubmed/25287733*. Copyright © 3 October 2013. All rights reserved.

p. 75/76: **Wheeler, Dr. David. Beaverton**, Oregon, USA. www. healthbreakthroughs.net

p. 84/85:   **Charles, R.H.** (ed.). *The Book of Enoch*. Bungay. 1917.

p. 92:   "Backing the Big Bang", by Alvin Powell, *Harvard Gazette*, 17 March 2014. All rights reserved.

p. 92/93:   "Water, Water Everywhere, Radio telescope finds water is common in universe", by Lee Simmons, *Harvard Gazette*, 25 February 1999. All rights reserved.

p. 101:   **Carroll, Lee and Tober, Jan**. *The Indigo Children. The New Kids Have Arrived.* Copyright © 1999. Published by Hay House, Inc., Carlsbad, CA, USA. All rights reserved.

p. 114:   **One Thought for World Peace** – *www.traceyash.com*

Bibliography

Angenot, Valence. *Horizon of Aten in Memphis.*Journal of the Society for the Study of Egyptian Antiquities, 35, 2005.

Bauval, Robert, and Adrian Gilbert. *The Orion Mystery*. New York: Crown Publishing, Inc., 1994.

Carroll, Lee & Tober, Jan. *The Indigo Children. The New Kids Have Arrived*. Hay House, 1999.

Cayce, Edgar Evans. *Edgar Cayce on Atlantis.*Grand Central Publishing, 1968.

Cox, Brian & Andrew Cohen.*Human Universe*. Collins, 2014.

Braden, Gregg. *Fractal Time*. Hay house, 2009.

Broadhurst, Paul & Miller, Hamish. *The Sun and The Serpent*. Mythos Press, 1989.

Budge, E. A. Wallis. *The Egyptian Book of The Dead.*Penguin Group. Penguin Classics, 2008.

Ions Review No 59. March-May 2002. *The Zero Point Field.*

Collins English Dictionary. HarperCollins Publishers, 2011.

Faulkner, Dr. Raymond & Dr Ogdon Goelet, Carol Andrews & James Wasserman. *The Egyptian Book of The Dead.The Book of Going Forth By Day*. Chronicle Books, 1994.

Freke, Tim & Gandy, Peter. *The Hermetica. The Lost Wisdom of the Pharaohs*. Penguin Group. Tarcher Edition, 1999.

Gagnon, John. *Message from The Ancients. The Great Pyramid and The Hudson Bay Pole*. Victor & Company, 2009.

Gardiner, Laurence. *Secrets of The Sacred Ark*. Element, 2003.

Gardiner, Philip with Osborn, Gary. *The Serpent Grail. The Truth Behind The Holy Grail. The Philosopher's Stone and The Elixir of Life*. Watkins Publishing, 2005.

Gardiner, Philip with Osborn, Gary. *The Shining Ones. The World's Most Powerful Secret Society Revealed*. Watkins Publishing, 2010.

Kemp, Barry. *The City of Akhenaton and Nefertiti. Amarna and Its People.* The American Universitiy Press in Cairo, 2012.

Hagan, Helene. E. *The Shining Ones.* Xilibris Corporation, 2000.

Hancock, Graham. *Finger Prints of The Gods. A Quest for the Beginning and the End.* Mandarin Paperback. 1996.

Hancock, Graham & Faiia, Santha. *Heaven's Mirror.Quest for The Lost Civilisation.*Penguin Books, 1999.

Hancock, Graham & Bauval, Robert. *Talisman. Sacred Cities, Secret Faith.* Penguin Group, 2004.

Narby, Jeremy. *The Cosmic Serpent. DNA and The Origins of Knowledge.* Phoenix and imprint of Orion Books, 1995.

Mehler, Stephen. S. *The Land of Osiris.* Adventures Unlimited Press, 2001.

Mehler, Stephen. S. *From Light into Darkness.* Adventures Unlimited Press, 2005.

Naydler, Jeremy. *Shamanic Wisdom in the Pyramid Texts, The Mystical Tradition of Ancient Egypt.*Inner Traditions, 2005.

Manniche. Lise. *The Akhenaton Colossi of Karnak.* The American University in Cairo Press, 2010.

McTaggart, Lynne. *The Field.* Element, 2001.

O'Briens. *Christian with Joy, the genius of The Few, The Story of Those who Founded The Garden of Eden.* Published by Dianthus Publishing, 1988. First published 1985.

Pevet, P. *Role of Melatonin, The internal time-giver, A key for our health.*

Picknett, Lynn & Clive Prince. *The Stargate Conspiracy.* Little, Brown & Company, 1999.

Roberts, Alison. *Hathor Rising. The Sepernt Power of Ancient Egypt.* Northgate Publishers, 1995.

Schwaller de Lubicz, R. A. *Esoterism & Symbolism.* Inner Traditions International,1985.

Schwaller de Lubicz, R. A. *Sacred Science. The King of Pharaonic Theocracy.* Inner Traditions International,1988.

Schwaller de Lubicz, R. A. *The Temple of Man.* Inner Traditions International, 1949.

Scrantin, Laird. *The Science of The Dogon. Decoding The African Mystery Tradition.* Inner Tradtions, 2002.

Suda, Gunji. *Rock Sanctuaries in Primeval Japan*. Gunji Suda, 2008.

Temple, Robert K. G. *The Sirius Mystery*. Rochester, VT:Destiny Books, 1987.

Vernon, David. *Human Potential. Exploring Techniques Used to Enhance Human Performance.*Routledge, 2009.

Wilcock, David. *The Hidden Science of Lost Civilisations. The Source Field Investigations*. Souvenir Press, 2011.

Wilkinson, Richard. H. *The Complete Gods and Goddesses of Ancient Egypt*. Thames and Hudson, 2003.

Websites of Interest

Below are a few websites that are well worth your visiting.

www.hcbi.nim.nih.gov
www.oed.com
www.pia-journal.co.uk
www.geology.com
www.gizapyramid.com
www.huffingtonpost.com
www.ions.org
www.nationalgeographic.com
www.melatoninresearch.org
www.mindunleashed.com
www.mosaicscience.com
www.oprah.com
www.pia-journal.co.uk
www.egyptsites.wordpress.com
www.fluoridealert.org
www.telegraph.com
www.superconsciousness.com
www.princeton.edu

Acknowledgements

I first thank my family, my very special daughters Scarlett and India Mae for your patience and support during our worldwide adventures exploring ancient sites and knowledge.

I am so grateful for the many discussions and kind words of support from all of my friends and family during the months of late summer and autumn 2014. I have spent so many weeks in my office and many precious weekends. I have sorely missed afternoon tea and long walks in the English countryside with my family.

Thank you for lovingly holding me with mugs of tea and delicious home-cooked food. My darling girls are growing into incredible inspirational young women. I also thank my parents for caring for my daughters during my travels.

I also acknowledge Sabine Weeke for introducing and welcoming me to the Findhorn Press stable of authors. I am deeply moved by the legacy of this organization. It feels so right for this book to belong with Findhorn. I am blessed to have such a magnificent organization supporting this project. I would like to thank everyone at the Findhorn Press team including Thierry Bogliolo, Carol Shaw, Mieke Wik, Elaine Harrison and Gail Torr. I also like to give divine gratitude to an amazing journey with Michael Hawkins, my brilliant editor.

I am deeply grateful to a long list of wonderful individuals and organizations who play or have played important roles in the inspiration, development and ongoing support of my work, research and writing in the UK and overseas. Three incredible women inspired me greatly.

One of these women, belongs to the magnificent legacy of mediumship of the last century. In 1993, I walked through the doors of the College of Psychic Studies on a sunny Saturday afternoon in South Kensington, to experience the outstanding mediumship of Ivy Northage. Her lecture on trance channelling and audience readings demonstrated her immense talent, in a full house, as she worked for so many of the audience.

Her detailed message to me confirmed my powerful childhood experiences and my journey to become a professional sensitive. I trained at the College of Psychic Studies and in 2000 was invited to work as a freelance consultant and lecturer by President Suzanna McInnery.

The second woman is Suzanna McInnery who became an incredible mentor for my work to come. Out of thousands who train at The College of Psychic Studies, few are invited to work. Under her guidance, I developed ground-breaking spirituality and awareness programmes for young adults at The College.

This created a think-tank and inspirational zone for the early pioneers and change-makers. This undoubtedly has been the inspirational heart of the work I do today. I have been utterly inspired by the level of excellence and have worked at The College of Psychic Studies since 2000.

And finally, Shirley MacLaine, for her outstanding and authentic contribution to the human potential movement, way ahead of the times. *Out on a Limb* magically inspired my journey to explore who I am and live for creating a better world.

I am so thankful to have these organizations and individuals in my life and destiny: Hiroko Imai and Natural Spirit will publish this book in Japan. Synchronicity Japan Inc for creating Psychic School Japan; Mt Fuji Peace Retreat, Life Vision School Japan and Celestial Healing and Life Vision consultations programmes. I give warmest thanks to CEO Masumi Hori and staff, in particular, Kyoko Fukazawa, Junko Haseyama, Meiko Sugawara and Sayaka Kai.

On New Year's Day 2011, I meditated for world peace on Glastonbury Tor and radiated my availability for service and contribution anywhere in the world. A couple of weeks later on a cold January afternoon, I took tea with Miyo Ichimura at the V&A in London and my contract to work in Japan was placed on the table!

I love being Synchronicity's number one teacher with a number one team! I also thank Catherine Cates for introducing me to PSI Science Institute Japan and Dr Kubota. It is a pleasure knowing and sharing with you, both at fascinating dinner parties and the papers we now share. I also acknowledge a long friendship with Violet Hill Studios, London and Pauline and Tony Groman, where my Life Vision School UK, Psychic School UK and Life Vision Readings are lovingly supported.

I also thank the support of Tree of Life Festival, Mind Body Soul Experience, Mind Body Spirit Festival, Natural Spirit Inc and Star People for supporting my presentations and magazine articles.

I also wish to express deep gratitude to Anthony Povah, Richard Dancer, Max Eammes, Tim Wheater, Caroline Horn, Marketa Bola, Joginder Bola, Linda Stevens and Andreas Thrasy, Jo White, Naoko Wantabe, Reiko Miharada, Nobu Matsuo, Newton and Angelini Oliveira, Sara Machado, Emma L. Gaywood,

Adrienne Levonian, John of God, The Spiritualist Association of Great Britain, The Theosophical Society, Isabel Brittain, Mariko Enright, The Conscious Network, Marie Eisl, The Yoga Show, Yoga life, Kindred Spirit, IONS, Richard Ward-Roden, Eileen Caddy, Carolyn Myss, The Dalai Lama, Arthur Conan-Doyle and Tracy West.

A very special thank you also, to support staff of Psychic School UK & Japan, Life Vision School UK & Japan, Celestial Healing School Japan, Conscious Retreats and Return to Light Tours Egypt; in particular Romany and Remon as superb Egyptologists.

And, not least, my love, gratitude and deep respect to all conscious individuals on this planet who are tirelessly working to shape new dreams of tomorrow for earth and humanity in this dramatic new world phase.

About Tracey Ash

Since 1999 more than fourteen thousand Life Vision consultations have been experienced by thought leaders, change influencers and conscious individuals worldwide, unlocking high-frequency purpose and pioneering contribution in world and communities. More than thirty thousand individuals have attended training in schools, retreats and expos. Tracey Ash is creator and founder of The Conscious Network, Conscious Retreats, Life Vision School, Psychic School and Celestial Healing. She is passionate about training excellence. She is an honorary member of PSI Science Institute Japan with accepted research papers on the subjects of consciousness and pioneering meditation technologies. She is currently leading research at PSI on science and benefits of world peace meditation. She has created a world-class library of film and photography archives during her journeys to ancient sites around the world documenting The Source Codes. She is passionate about understanding miracles of human consciousness and contribution. *She believes miracles of consciousness are now urgently required for critical positive planetary and humanity change. This urgent change starts at grass roots level with those individuals willing to transform and create change.*

Tracey Ash reveals truths on 'how to' change and enhance important stories, re-framing potential in essential peace and awareness. She designs groundbreaking meditation technologies, transformation and manifestation processes, high-frequency living approaches, new humanity and planetary healing templates. She researches our cosmic origins via ancient monuments, alternative history and new spirituality. She explores the possibilities of journeys in high-frequency mission and action that create a better world. She is a passionate change-maker for a world of solutions and peace for our future generations. A maverick pioneer and researcher in a new frontier of super-consciousness, Tracey cuts through the illusion and wasted time served up by pain and conflict cycles addiction and poor energy approaches that distract your magnificence and outstanding purpose. Tracey is a high-frequency master technician, manoeuvering and modifying limiting stories fast in resolution. She is a dedicated world-class teacher, sharing groundbreaking technologies on healing, awareness and manifestation excellence for every day. She is an outstanding life purpose visionary, often working over thousands of miles by Skype with translators giving astonishing information that creates miracle change in people's lives. She is passionate about listening and unlocking magnificent stories that really matter. She is committed to making a difference and helping others to create better lives and worlds.

From 1999, Life Vision consultations have led the way in high-frequency life purpose and outstanding contribution of visionaries of positive change. Tracey has worked with thousands of conscious individuals, pioneers in business and Hollywood visionaries. Psychic School and Life Vision School were created in London, Tokyo and Lisbon to deliver outstanding awareness and human potential training. Conscious Retreats are held at earth power sites, ancient monuments and deserts of Egypt, Mount Fuji and Europe for outstanding high-frequency transformation, awareness and manifestation. With Ahmed, they create horse-riding journeys exploring powerful inner transformation in the silence of the desert amidst the ancient monuments of Egypt. Tracey Ash is a presenter, teacher, writer and consultant, appearing at Synchronicity Inc Japan, College of Psychic Studies, Tree of Life Festival, Mind Body Soul Experience, Natural Spirit, Dynavision, The Yoga Show, PSI Science Institute Japan, Mind Body Spirit Festival, London Wellbeing Festival, London College of Spirituality and Findhorn Press. Media and other writing includes, Channel Four, Cutting Edge, Radio Four, Five Live, The Daily Express, The Evening Standard, Yoga Life, The Mother, The Daily Mirror, The Guardian, Kindred Spirit, Star People, and PSI Science Journal.

She lives in a quiet village in rural England with her family. She loves research, travel, good conversation and horse riding in The Sahara between the ancient pyramids of Egypt. She will travel impressive distances for Japan's onsen (or hot springs), quirky vintage and antiques eccentricity and, of course, journeys to ancient power sites. Her greatest passion is sharing knowledge on how to achieve excellence, outstanding awareness and positive change in all that we do. She shares her time between UK, Egypt and Japan working with incredible individuals.

www.traceyash.com

http://youtu.be/-UkdAKkDErE
The Source Codes, Egypt, Film Archive 2011.
www.youtube.com/user/awakeningsystem

FINDHORN PRESS

Life-Changing Books

Consult our catalogue online
(with secure order facility) on
www.findhornpress.com

For information on the Findhorn Foundation:
www.findhorn.org